John M. Synge

In Wicklow and West Kerry

weitsuechtig

John M. Synge

In Wicklow and West Kerry

ISBN/EAN: 9783956560323

Auflage: 1

Erscheinungsjahr: 2013

Erscheinungsort: Bremen, Deutschland

@ weitsuechtig in Access Verlag GmbH. Alle Rechte beim Verlag und bei den jeweiligen Lizenzgebern.

Cover: Foto © Eirian Evans (Wikipedia)

weitsuechtig

Contents

IN WICKLOW	1
The Oppression of the Hills	10
On the Road	15
The People of the Glens	20
AT A WICKLOW FAIR	31
A Landlord's Garden in County Wicklow	37
Glencree	42
In West Kerry	46

IN WICKLOW

The Vagrants of Wicklow

Some features of County Wicklow, such as the position of the principal workhouses and holiday places on either side of the coach road from Arklow to Bray, have made this district a favourite with the vagrants of Ireland. A few of these people have been on the roads for generations; but fairly often they seem to have merely drifted out from the ordinary people of the villages, and do not differ greatly from the class they come from. Their abundance has often been regretted; yet in one sense it is an interesting sign, for wherever the labourer of a country has preserved his vitality, and begets an occasional temperament of distinction, a certain number of vagrants are to be looked for. In the middle classes the gifted son of a family is always the poorest — usually a writer or artist with no sense for speculation — and in a family of peasants, where the average comfort is just over penury, the gifted son sinks also, and is soon a tramp on the roadside.

In this life, however, there are many privileges. The tramp in Ireland is little troubled by the laws, and lives in out-of-door conditions that keep him in good-humour and fine bodily health. This is so apparent, in Wicklow at least, that these men rarely seek for charity on any plea of ill-health, but ask simply, when they beg: 'Would you help a poor fellow along the road?' or, 'Would you give me the price of a night's lodging, for I'm after walking a great way since the sun rose?'

The healthiness of this life, again, often causes people to live to a great age, though it is not always easy to test the stories that are told of their longevity. One man, however, who died not long ago, claimed to have reached one hundred and two with a show of likelihood; for several old people remember his first appearance in a certain district as a man of middle age, about the year of the Famine, in 1847 or 1848. This man could hardly be classed with ordinary tramps, for he was married several times in different parts of the world, and reared children of whom he seemed to have forgotten, in his old age, even the names and sex. In his early life he spent thirty years at sea, where he sailed with some one he spoke of afterwards as 'Il mio capitane,' visiting India and Japan, and gaining odd words and intonations that gave colour to his language. When he was too old to wander in the world, he learned all the paths of Wicklow, and till the end of his life he could go the thirty miles from Dublin to the Seven Churches without, as he said, 'putting out his foot on a white road, or seeing any Christian but the hares and moon.' When he was over ninety he married an old woman of eighty-five. Before many days, however, they quarrelled so fiercely that he beat her with his stick, and came out again on the roads. In a few hours he was arrested at her complaint, and sentenced to a month in Kuilmainham. He cared nothing for the plank-bed and uncomfortable diet; but he always gathered himself together, and cursed with extraordinary rage, as he told how they had cut off the white hair which had grown down upon his shoulders. All his pride and his half-conscious feeling for the dignity of his age seemed to have set themselves on this long hair, which marked him out from the other people of his district; and I have often heard him saying to himself, as he sat beside me under a ditch: 'What use is an old man without his hair? A man has only his bloom like the trees; and what use is an old man without his white hair?'

Among the country people of the east of Ireland the tramps and tinkers who wander round from the west have a curious reputation for witchery and unnatural powers. 'There's great witchery in that country,' a man said to me once, on the side of a mountain to the east of Aughavanna, in Wicklow. 'There's great witchery in that country, and great knowledge of the fairies. I've had men lodging with me out of the west — men who would be walking the world looking for a bit of money — and every one of them would be talking of the wonders below in Connemara. I remember one time, a while after I was married, there was a tinker down there in the glen, and two women along with him. I brought him into my cottage to do a bit of a job, and my first child was there lying in the bed, and he covered up to his chin with the bed-clothes. When the tallest of the women came in, she looked around at him, and then she says:

"That's a fine boy, God bless him."

"How do you know it's a boy," says my woman, "when it's only the head of him you see?"

"I know rightly," says the tinker, "and it's the

first too."

'Then my wife was going to slate me for bringing in people to bewitch the child, and I had to turn the lot of them out to finish the job in the lane.'

I asked him where most of the tinkers came from that are met with in Wicklow. 'They come from every part,' he said. 'They're gallous lads for walking round through the world. One time I seen fifty of them above on the road to Rathdangan, and they all matchmaking and marrying themselves for the year that was to come. One man would take such a woman, and say he was going such roads and places, stopping at this fair and another fair, till he'd meet them again at such a place, when the spring was coming on. Another, maybe, would swap the woman he had with one from another man, with as much talk as if you'd be selling a cow. It's two hours I was there watching them from the bog underneath, where I was cutting turf and the like of the crying and kissing, and the singing and the shouting began when they went off this way and that way, you never heard in your life. Sometimes when a party would be gone a bit down over the hill, a girl would begin crying out and wanting to go back to her ma. Then the man would say: "Black hell to your soul, you've come with me now, and you'll go the whole way." I often seen tinkers before and since, but I never seen such a power of them as were in it that day.'

It need hardly be said that in all tramp life plaintive and tragic elements are common, even on the surface. Some are peculiar to Wicklow. In these hills the summer passes in a few weeks from a late spring, full of odour and colour, to an autumn that is premature and filled with the desolate splendour of decay; and it often happens that, in moments when one is most aware of this ceaseless fading of beauty, some incident of tramp life gives a local human intensity to the shadow of one's own mood.

One evening, on the high ground near the Avonbeg, I met a young tramp just as an extraordinary sunset had begun to fade, and a low white mist was rising from the bogs. He had a sort of table in his hands that he seemed to have made himself out of twisted rushes and a few branches of osier. His clothes were more than usually ragged, and I could see by his face that he was suffering from some terrible disease. When he was quite close, he held out the table.

'Would you give me a few pence for that thing?' he said. 'I'm after working at it all day by the river, and for the love of God give me something now, the way I can get a drink and lodging for the night.'

I felt in my pockets, and could find nothing but a shilling piece.

'I wouldn't wish to give you so much,' I said, holding it out to him, 'but it is all I have, and I don't like to give you nothing at all, and the darkness coming on. Keep the table; it's no use to me, and you'll maybe sell it for something in the morning.'

The shilling was more than he expected, and his eyes flamed with joy.

'May the Almighty God preserve you and

watch over you and reward you for this night,' he said, 'but you'll take the table; I wouldn't keep it at all, and you after stretching out your hand with a shilling to me, and the darkness coming on.'

He forced it into my hands so eagerly that I could not refuse it, and set off down the road with tottering steps. When he had gone a few yards, I called after him: 'There's your table; take it and God speed you.'

Then I put down his table on the ground, and set off as quickly as I was able. In a moment he came up with me, holding the table in his hands, and slipped round in front of me so that I could not get away.

'You wouldn't refuse it,' he said, 'and I after working at it all day below by the river.'

He was shaking with excitement and the exertion of overtaking me; so I took his table and let him go on his way. A quarter of a mile further on I threw it over the ditch in a desolate place, where no one was likely to find it.

In addition to the more genuine vagrants a number of wandering men and women are to be met with in the northern parts of the county, who walk out for ferns and flowers in bands of from four or five to a dozen. They usually set out in the evening, and sleep in some ditch or shed, coming home the next night with what they have gathered. If their sales are successful, both men and women drink heavily; so that they are always on the edge of starvation, and are miserably dressed, the women sometimes wearing nothing but an old petticoat and shawl — a scantiness of clothing that is sometimes met with also among the road-women of Kerry.

These people are nearly always at war with the police, and are often harshly treated. Once after a holiday, as I was walking home through a village on the border of Wicklow, I came upon several policemen, with a crowd round them, trying to force a drunken flower-woman out of the village. She did not wish to go, and threw herself down, raging and kicking on the ground. They let her lie there for a few moments, and then she propped herself up against the wall, scolding and storming at every one, till she became so outrageous the police renewed their attack. One of them walked up to her and hit her a sharp blow on the jaw with the back of his hand. Then two more of them seized her by the shoulders and forced her along the road for a few yards, till her clothes began to tear off with the violence of the struggle, and they let her go once more.

She sprang up at once when they did so. 'Let this be the barrack's yard, if you wish it,' she cried out, tearing off the rags that still clung about her. 'Let this be the barrack's yard, and come on now, the lot of you.'

Then she rushed at them with extraordinary fury; but the police, to avoid scandal, withdrew into the town, and left her to be quieted by her friends.

Sometimes, it is fair to add, the police are generous and good-humoured. One evening, many years ago, when Whit-Monday in Enniskerry was a very different thing from what it is now, I was looking out of a window in that village, watching the police, who had been brought in for the occasion, getting ready to start for Bray. As they were standing about, a young ballad-singer came along from the Dargle, and one of the policemen, who seemed to know him, asked him why a fine, stout lad the like of him wasn't earning his bread, instead of straying on the roads.

Immediately the young man drew up on the spot where he was, and began shouting a loud ballad at the top of his voice. The police tried to stop him; but he went on, getting faster and faster, till he ended, swinging his head from side to side, in a furious patter, of which I seem to remember —

Botheration
Take the nation,
Calculation,
In the stable,
Cain and Abel,
Tower of Babel,
And the Battle of Waterloo.

Then he pulled off his hat, dashed in among the police, and did not leave them till they had all given him the share of money he felt he had earned for his bread.

In all the circumstances of this tramp life there is a certain wildness that gives it romance and a peculiar value for those who look at life in Ireland with an eye that is aware of the arts also. In all the healthy movements of art, variations from the ordinary types of manhood are made interesting for the ordinary man, and in this way only the higher arts are universal. Beside this art, however, founded on the variations which are a condition and effect of all vigorous life, there is another art — sometimes confounded with it — founded on the freak of nature, in itself a mere sign of atavism or disease. This latter art, which is occupied with the antics of the freak, is of interest only to the variation from ordinary minds, and for this reason is never universal. To be quite plain, the tramp in real life, Hamlet and Faust in the arts, are variations; but the maniac in real life, and Des Esseintes and all his ugly crew in the arts, are freaks only.

The Oppression of the Hills

AMONG the cottages that are scattered through the hills of County Wicklow I have met with many people who show in a singular way the influence of a particular locality. These people live for the most part beside old roads and pathways where hardly one man passes in the day, and look out all the year on unbroken barriers of heath. At every season heavy rains fall for often a week at a time, till the thatch drips with water stained to a dull chestnut, and the floor in the cottages seems to be going back to the condition of the bogs near it. Then the clouds break, and there is a night of terrific storm from the south-west — all the larches that survive in these places are bowed and twisted towards the point where the sun rises in June — when the winds come down through the narrow glens with the congested whirl and roar of a torrent, breaking at times for sudden moments of silence that keep up the tension of the mind. At such times the people crouch all night over a few sods of turf and the dogs howl, in the lanes.

When the sun rises there is a morning of almost supernatural radiance, and even the oldest men and women come out into the air with the joy of children who have recovered from a fever. In the evening it is raining again. This peculiar climate, acting on a population that is already lonely and dwindling, has caused or increased a tendency to nervous depression among the people, and every degree of sadness, from that of the man who is merely mournful to that of the man who has spent half his life in the madhouse, is common among these hills.

Not long ago in a desolate glen in the south of the county I met two policemen driving an ass-cart with a coffin on it, and a little further on I stopped an old man and asked him what had happened.

'This night three weeks,' he said, 'there was a poor fellow below reaping in the glen, and in the evening he had two glasses of whisky with some other lads. Then some excitement took him, and he threw off his clothes and ran away into the hills. There was great rain that night, and I suppose the poor creature lost his way, and was the whole night perishing in the rain and darkness. In the morning they found his naked footmarks on some mud half a mile above the road, and again where you go up by a big stone. Then there was nothing known of him till last night, when they found his body on the mountain, and it near eaten by the crows.'

Then he went on to tell me how different the country had been when he was a young man.

'We had nothing to eat at that time,' he said, 'but milk and stirabout and potatoes, and there was a fine constitution you wouldn't meet this day at all. I remember when you'd see forty boys and girls below there on a Sunday evening, playing ball and diverting themselves; but now all this country is gone lonesome and bewildered, and there's no man knows what ails it.'

There are so few girls left in these neighbourhoods that one does not often meet with women that have grown up unmarried. I know one, however, who has lived by herself for fifteen years in a tiny hovel near a cross roads much frequented by tinkers and ordinary tramps. As she has no one belonging to her, she spends a good deal of her time wandering through the country, and I have met her in every direction, often many miles from her own glen. 'I do be so afeard of the tramps,' she said to me one evening. 'I live all alone, and what would I do at all if one of them lads was to come near me? When my poor mother was dying, "Now, Nanny," says she, "don't be living on here when I am dead," says she; "it'd be too lonesome." And now I wouldn't wish to go again' my mother, and she dead — dead or alive I wouldn't go again' my mother — but I'm after doing all I can, and I can't get away by any means.' As I was moving on she heard, or thought she heard, a sound of distant thunder.

'Ah, your honour,' she said, 'do you think it's thunder we'll be having? There's nothing I fear like the thunder. My heart isn't strong — I do feel it — and I have a lightness in my head, and often when I do be excited with the thunder I do be afeard I might die there alone in the cottage and no one know it. But I do hope that the Lord — bless His holy name! — has something in store for me. I've done all I can, and I don't like going again' my mother and she dead. And now good evening, your honour, and safe home.'

Intense nervousness is common also with much younger women. I remember one night hearing some one crying out and screaming in the house where I was staying. I went downstairs and found it was a girl who had been taken in from a village a few miles away to help the servants. That afternoon her two younger sisters had come to see her, and now she had been taken with a panic that they had been drowned going home through the bogs, and she was crying and wailing, and saying she must go to look for them. It was not thought fit for her to leave the house alone so late in the evening, so I went with her. As we passed down a steep hill of heather, where the nightjars were clapping their wings in the moonlight, she told me a long story of the way she had been frightened. Then we reached a solitary cottage on the edge of the bog, and as a light was still shining in the window, I knocked at the door and asked if they had seen or heard anything. When they understood our errand three half-dressed generations came out to jeer at us on the doorstep.

'Ah, Maggie,' said the old woman, 'you're a cute one. You're the girl likes a walk in the moonlight. Whist your talk of them big lumps of childer, and look at Martin Edward there, who's not six, and he can go through the bog five times in an hour and not wet his feet.'

My companion was still unconvinced, so we went on. The rushes were shining in the moonlight, and one flake of mist was lying on the river. We looked into one bog-hole, and then into another, where a snipe rose and terrified us. We listened: a cow was chewing heavily in the shadow of a bush, two dogs were barking on the side of a hill, and there was a cart far away upon the road. Our teeth began to chatter with the cold of the bog air and the loneliness of the night. I could see that the actual presence of the bog had shown my companion the absurdity of her fears, and in a little while we went home.

The older people in County Wicklow, as in the rest of Ireland, still show a curious affection for the landed classes wherever they have lived for a generation or two upon their property. I remember an old woman, who told me, with tears streaming on her face, how much more lonely the country had become since the 'quality' had gone away, and gave me a long story of how she had seen her landlord shutting up his house and leaving his property, and of the way he had died afterwards, when the 'grievance' of it broke his heart. The younger people feel differently, and when I was passing this landlord's house, not long afterwards, I found these lines written in pencil on the door-post:

In the days of rack-renting
And land-grabbing so vile
A proud, heartless landlord
Lived here a great while.
When the League it was started,
And the land-grabbing cry,
To the cold North of Ireland
He had for to fly.

A year later the door-post had fallen to pieces, and the inscription with it.

On the Road

ONE evening after heavy rains I set off to walk to a village at the other side of some hills, part of my way lying along a steep heathery track. The valleys that I passed through were filled with the strange splendour that comes after wet weather in Ireland, and on the tops of the mountains masses of fog were lying in white, even banks. Once or twice I went by a lonely cottage with a smell of earthy turf coming from the chimney, weeds or oats sprouting on the thatch, and a broken cart before the door, with many straggling hens going to roost on the shafts. Near these cottages little bands of half-naked children, filled with the excitement of evening, were running and screaming over the bogs, where the heather was purple already, giving me the strained feeling of regret one has so often in these places when there is rain in the air.

Further on, as I was going up a long hill, an old man with a white, pointed face and heavy beard pulled himself up out of the ditch and joined me. We spoke first about the broken weather, and then he began talking in a mournful voice of the famines and misfortunes that have been in Ireland.

'There have been three cruel plagues,' he said, 'out through the country since I was born in the west. First, there was the big wind in 1839, that tore away the grass and green things from the earth. Then there was the blight that came on the 9th of June in the year 1846. Up to then the potatoes were clean and good; but that morning a mist rose up out of the sea, and you could hear a voice talking near a mile off across the stillness of the earth. It was the same the next day, and the day after, and so on for three days or more; and then you could begin to see the tops of the stalks lying over as if the life was gone out of them. And that was the beginning of the great trouble and famine that destroyed Ireland. Then the people went on, I suppose, in their wickedness and their animosity of one against the other; and the Almighty God sent down the third plague, and that was the sickness called the choler. Then all the people left the town of Sligo — it's in Sligo I was reared — and you could walk through the streets at the noon of day and not see a person, and you could knock at one door and another door and find no one to answer you. The people were travelling out north and south and east, with the terror that was on them; and the country people were digging ditches across the roads and driving them back where they could, for they had great dread of the disease.

'It was the law at that time that if there was sickness on any person in the town of Sligo you should notice it to the Governors, or you'd be put up in the gaol. Well, a man's wife took sick, and he went and noticed it. They came down then with bands of men they had, and took her away to the sick-house, and he heard nothing more till he heard she was dead, and was to be buried in the morning. At that time there was such fear and hurry and dread on every person, they were burying people they had no hope of, and they with life within them. My man was uneasy a while thinking on that, and then what did he do, but slip down in the darkness of the night and into the dead-house, where they were after putting his wife. There were beyond twoscore bodies, and he went feeling from one to the other. Then I suppose his wife heard him coming — she wasn't dead at all — and "Is that Michael?" says she. "It is then," says he; "and, oh, my poor woman, have you your last gasps in you still?" "I have, Michael," says she; "and they're after setting me out here with fifty bodies the way they'll put me down into my grave at the dawn of day." "Oh, my poor woman," says he; "have you the strength left in you to hold on my back?" "Oh, Micky," says she, "I have surely." He took her up then on his back, and he carried her out by lanes and tracks till he got to his house. Then he never let on a word about it, and at the end of three days she began to pick up, and in a month's time she came out and began walking about like yourself or me. And there were many people were afeard to speak to her, for they thought she was after coming back from the grave.'

Soon afterwards we passed into a little village, and he turned down a lane and left me. It was not long, however, till another old man that I could see a few paces ahead stopped and waited for me, as is the custom of the place.

'I've been down in Kilpeddar buying a scythe-stone,' he began, when I came up to him, 'and indeed Kilpeddar is a dear place, for it's three-pence they charged me for it; but I suppose there must be a profit from every trade, and we must all live and let live.'

When we had talked a little more I asked him if he had been often in Dublin.

'I was living in Dublin near ten years,' he said; 'and indeed I don't know what way I lived that length in it, for there is no place with smells like the city of Dublin. One time I went up with my wife into those lanes where they sell old clothing, Hanover Lane and Plunket's Lane, and when my wife — she's dead now, God forgive her! — when my wife smelt the dirty air she put her apron up to her nose, and, "For the love of God," says she, "get me away out of this place." And now may I ask if it's from there you are yourself, for I think by your speaking it wasn't in these parts you were reared?'

I told him I was born in Dublin, but that I had travelled afterwards and been in Paris and Rome, and seen the Pope Leo XIII.

'And will you tell me,' he said, 'is it true that anyone at all can see the Pope?'

I described the festivals in the Vatican, and how I had seen the Pope carried through long halls on a sort of throne. 'Well, now,' he said, 'can you tell me who was the first Pope that sat upon that throne?'

I hesitated for a moment, and he went on:

'I'm only a poor, ignorant man, but I can tell you that myself if you don't know it, with all your travels. Saint Peter was the first Pope, and he was crucified with his head down, and since that time there have been Popes upon the throne of Rome.'

Then he began telling me about himself.

'I was twice a married man,' he said. 'My first wife died at her second child, and then I reared it up till it was as tall as myself — a girl it was — and she went off and got married and left me. After that I was married a second time to an aged woman, and she lived with me ten year; and then she died herself. There is nothing I can make now but tea, and tea is killing me; and I'm living alone, in a little hut beyond, where four baronies, four parishes, and four townlands meet.'

By this time we had reached the village inn, where I was lodging for the night; so I stood him a drink, and he went on to his cottage along a narrow pathway through the bogs.

The People of the Glens

HERE and there in County Wicklow there are a number of little known places — places with curiously melodious names, such as Aughavanna, Glenmalure, Annamoe, or Lough Nahanagan — where the people have retained a peculiar simplicity, and speak a language in some ways more Elizabethan than the English of Connaught, where Irish was used till a much later date. In these glens many women still wear old-fashioned bonnets, with a frill round the face, and the old men, when they are going to the fair, or to Mass, are often seen in curiously-cut frock-coats, tall hats, and breeches buckled at the knee. When they meet a wanderer on foot, these old people are glad to stop and talk to him for hours, telling him stories of the Rebellion, or of the fallen angels that ride across the hills, or alluding to the three shadowy countries that are never forgotten in Wicklow — America (their El Dorado), the Union and the Madhouse.

'I had a power of children,' an old man who was born in Glenmalure said to me once; 'I had a power of children, and they all went to California, with what I could give them, and bought a bit of a field. Then, when they put in the plough, it stuck fast on them. They looked in beneath it, and there was fine gold stretched within the earth. They're rich now and their daughters are riding on fine horses with new saddles on them and elegant bits in their mouths, yet not a ha'porth did they ever send me, and may the devil ride with them to hell!'

Not long afterwards I met an old man wandering about a hill-side, where there was a fine view of Lough Dan, in extraordinary excitement and good spirits.

'I landed in Liverpool two days ago,' he said, when I had wished him the time of day; 'then I came to the city of Dublin this morning, and took the train to Bray, where you have the blue salt water on your left, and the beautiful valleys, with trees in them, on your right. From that I drove to this place on a jaunting-car to see some brothers and cousins I have living below. They're poor people, Mister honey, with bits of cabins, and mud floors under them, but they're as happy as if they were in heaven, and what more would a man want than that? In America and Australia, and on the Atlantic Ocean, you have all sorts, good people and bad people, and murderers and thieves, and pickpockets; but in this place there isn't a being isn't as good and decent as yourself or me.'

I saw he was one of the old people one sometimes meets with who emigrated when the people were simpler than they are at present, and who often come back, after a lifetime in the States, as Irish as any old man who has never been twenty miles from the town of Wicklow. I asked him about his life abroad, when we had talked a little longer.

'I've been through perils enough to slay nations,' he said, 'and the people here think I should be rotten with gold, but they're better off the way they are. For five years I was a ship's smith, and never saw dry land, and I in all the danger and peril of the Atlantic Ocean. Then I was a veterinary surgeon, curing side-slip, splay-foot, spavin, splints, glanders, and the various ailments of the horse and ass. The lads in this place think you've nothing to do but to go across the sea and fill a bag with gold; but I tell you it is hard work, and in those countries the workhouses is full, and the prisons is full, and the crazy-houses is full, the same as in the city of Dublin. Over beyond you have fine dwellings, and you have only to put out your hand from the window among roses and vines, and the red wine grape; but there is all sorts in it, and the people is better in this country, among the trees and valleys, and they resting on their floors of mud.'

In Wicklow, as in the rest of Ireland, the union, though it is a home of refuge for the tramps and tinkers, is looked on with supreme horror by the peasants. The madhouse, which they know better, is less dreaded.

One night I had to go down late in the evening from a mountain village to the town of Wicklow, and come back again into the hills. As soon as I came near Rathnew I passed many bands of girls and men making rather ruffianly flirtation on the pathway, and women who surged up to stare at me, as I passed in the middle of the road. The thick line of trees that are near Rathnew makes the way intensely dark even on clear nights, and when one is riding quickly, the contrast, when one reaches the lights of Wicklow, is singularly abrupt. The town itself after nightfall is gloomy and squalid. Half-drunken men and women stand about, wrangling and disputing in the dull light from the windows, which is only strong enough to show the wretchedness of the figures which pass continually across them. I did my business quickly and turned back to the hills, passing for the first few miles the same noisy groups and couples on the roadway. After a while I stopped at a lonely public-house to get a drink and rest for a moment before I came to the hills. Six or seven men were talking drearily at one end of the room, and a woman I knew, who had been marketing in Wicklow, was resting nearer the door. When I had been given a glass of beer, I sat down on a barrel near her, and we began to talk.

'Ah, your honour,' she said, 'I hear you're going off in a short time to Dublin, or to France, and maybe we won't be in the place at all when you come back. There's no fences to the bit of farm I have, the way I'm destroyed running. The calves do be straying, and the geese do be straying, and the hens do be straying, and I'm destroyed running after them. We've no man in the place since himself died in the winter, and he ailing these five years, and there's no one to give us a hand drawing the hay or cutting the bit of oats we have above on the hill. My brother Michael has come back to his own place after being seven years in the Richmond Asylum; but what can you ask of him, and he with a long family of his own? And, indeed, it's a wonder he ever came back when it was a fine time he had in the asylum.'

She saw my movement of surprise, and went on:

'There was a son of my own, as fine a lad as you'd see in the county — though I'm his mother that says it, and you'd never think it t look at me.

Well, he was a keeper in a kind of private asylum, I think they call it, and when Michael was taken bad, he went to see him, and didn't he know the keepers that were in charge of him, and they promised to take the best of care of him, and, indeed, he was always a quiet man that would give no trouble. After the first three years he was free in the place, and he walking about like a gentleman, doing any light work he'd find agreeable. Then my son went to see him a second time, and "You'll never see Michael again," says he when he came back, "for he's too well off where he is." And, indeed, it was well for him, but now he's come home.' Then she got up to carry out some groceries she was buying to the ass-cart that was waiting outside.

'It's real sorry I do be when I see you going off' she said, as she was turning away. 'I don't often speak to you, but it's company to see you passing up and down over the hill, and now may the Almighty God bless and preserve you, and see you safe home.'

A little later I was walking up the long hill which leads to the high ground from Laragh to Sugar Loaf. The solitude was intense. Towards the top of the hill I passed through a narrow gap with high rocks on one side of it and fir trees above them, and a handful of jagged sky filled with extraordinarily brilliant stars. In a few moments I passed out on the brow of the hill that runs behind the Devil's Glen, and smelt the fragrance of the bogs. I mounted again. There was not light enough to show the mountains round me, and the earth seemed to have dwindled away into a mere platform where an astrologer might watch. Among these emotions of the

24

night one cannot wonder that the madhouse is so often named in Wicklow.

Many of the old people of the country, however, when they have no definite sorrow, are not mournful, and are full of curious whims and observations. One old woman who lived near Glen Macanass told me that she had seen her sons had no hope of making a livelihood in the place where they were born, so, in addition to their schooling, she engaged a master to come over the bogs every evening and teach them sums and spelling. One evening she came in behind them, when they were at work, and stopped to listen.

'And what do you think my son was after doing?' she said; 'he'd made a sum of how many times a wheel on a cart would turn round between the bridge below and the Post Office in Dublin. Would you believe that? I went out without saying a word, and I got the old stocking, where I keep a bit of money, and I made out what I owed the master. Then I went in again, and "Master," says I, "Mick's learning enough for the likes of him. You can go now and safe home to you." And, God bless you, avourneen, Mick got a fine job after on the railroad.'

Another day, when she was trying to flatter me, she said: 'Ah, God bless you, avourneen, you've no pride. Didn't I hear you yesterday, and you talking to my pig below in the field as if it was your brother? And a nice clean pig it is too, the crathur.' A year or two afterwards I met this old woman again. Her husband had died a few months before of the 'Influence,' and she was in pitiable distress, weeping and wailing while she talked to me. 'The poor old man is after dying on me,' she said, 'and he was great company. There's only one son left me now, and we do be killed working. Ah, avourneen, the poor do have great stratagems to keep in their little cabins at all. And did you ever see the like of the place we live in? Isn't it the poorest, lonesomest, wildest, dreariest bit of a hill a person ever passed a life on?' When she stopped a moment, with the tears streaming on her face, I told a little about the poverty I had seen in Paris. 'God Almighty forgive me, avourneen,' she went on, when I had finished, 'we don't know anything about it. We have our bit of turf, and our bit of sticks, and our bit to eat, and we have our health. Glory be to His Holy Name, not a one of the childer was ever a day ill, except one boy was hurted off a cart, and he never overed it. It's small right we have to complain at all.'

She died the following winter, and her son went to New York.

The old people who have direct tradition of the Rebellion, and a real interest in it, are growing less numerous daily, but one still meets with them here and there in the more remote districts.

One evening, at the beginning of harvest, as I was walking into a straggling village, far away in the mountains, in the southern half of the county, I overtook an old man walking in the same direction with an empty gallon can. I joined him; and when we had talked for a moment, he turned round and looked at me curiously.

'Begging your pardon, sir,' he said, 'I think you

aren't Irish.' I told him he was mistaken.

'Well,' he went on, 'you don't speak the same as we do; so I was thinking maybe you were from another country.'

'I came back from France,' I said, 'two months ago, and maybe there's a trace of the language still upon my tongue.' He stopped and beamed with satisfaction.

'Ah,' he said, 'see that now. I knew there was something about you. I do be talking to all who do pass through this glen, telling them stories of the Rebellion, and the old histories of Ireland, and there's few can puzzle me, though I'm only a poor ignorant man.' He told me some of his adventures, and then he stopped again.

'Look at me now,' he said, 'and tell me what age you think I'd be.'

'You might be seventy,' I said.

'Ah,' he said, with a piteous whine in his voice, 'you wouldn't take me to be as old as that? No man ever thought me that age to this day.'

'Maybe you aren't far over sixty,' I said, fearing I had blundered; 'maybe you're sixty-four.' He beamed once more with delight, and hurried along the road.

'Go on, now,' he said, 'I'm eighty-two years, three months and five days. Would you believe that? I was baptized on the fourth of June, eighty-two years ago, and it's the truth I'm telling you.'

'Well, it's a great wonder,' I said, 'to think you're that age, when you're as strong as I am to this day.'

'I am not strong at all,' he went on, more despondingly, 'not strong the way I was. If I had two glasses of whisky I'd dance a hornpipe would dazzle your eyes; but the way I am at this minute you could knock me down with a rush. I have a noise in my head, so that you wouldn't hear the river at the side of it, and I can't sleep at nights. It's that weakens me. I do be lying in the darkness thinking of all that has happened in three-score years to the families of Wicklow — what this son did, and what that son did, and of all that went across the sea, and wishing black hell would seize them that never wrote three words to say were they alive or in good health. That's the profession I have now — to be thinking of all the people, and of the times that's gone. And, begging your pardon, might I ask your name?'

I told him.

'There are two branches of the Synges in the County Wicklow,' he said, and then he went on to tell me fragments of folk-lore connected with my forefathers. How a lady used to ride through Roundwood 'on a curious beast' to visit an uncle of hers in Roundwood Park, and how she married one of the Synges and got her weight in gold — eight stone of gold — as her dowry stories that referred to events which took place more than a hundred years ago.

When he had finished I told him how much I wondered at his knowledge of the country.

'There's not a family I don't know,' he said,

'from Baltinglass to the sea, and what they've done, and who they've married. You don't know me yet, but if you were a while in this place talking to myself, it's more pleasure and gratitude you'd have from my company than you'd have maybe from many a gentleman you'd meet riding or driving a car.'

By this time we had reached a wayside public-house, where he was evidently going with his can, so, as I did not wish to part with him so soon, I asked him to come in and take something with me. When we went into the little bar-room, which was beautifully clean, I asked him what he would have. He turned to the publican:

'Have you any good whisky at the present time?' he said.

'Not now, nor at any time,' said the publican, 'we only keep bad; but isn't it all the same for the likes of you that wouldn't know the difference?'

After prolonged barging he got a glass of whisky, took off his hat before he tasted it, to say a prayer for my future, and then sat down with it on a bench in the corner.

I was served in turn, and we began to talk about horses and racing, as there had been races in Arklow a day or two before. I alluded to some races I had seen in France, and immediately the publican's wife, a young woman who had just come in, spoke of a visit she had made to the Grand Prix a few years before.

'Then you have been in France?' I asked her.

'For eleven years,' she replied.

'Alors vous parlez Francais, Madame?'

'Mais oui, Monsieur,' she answered with pure intonation.

We had a little talk in French, and then the old man got his can filled with porter — the evening drink for a party of reapers who were working on the hill — bought a pennyworth of sweets, and went back down the road.

'That's the greatest old rogue in the village,' said the publican, as soon as he was out of hearing; 'he's always making up to all who pass through the place, and trying what he can get out of them. The other day a party told me to give him a bottle of XXX porter he was after asking for. I just gave him the dregs of an old barrel we had finished, and there he was, sucking in his lips, and saying it was the finest drink ever he tasted, and that it was rising to his head already, though he'd hardly a drop of it swallowed. Faith, in the end I had to laugh to hear the talk he was making.'

A little later I wished them good evening and started again on my walk, as I had two mountains to cross.

AT A WICKLOW FAIR

The Place and the People

A YEAR or two ago I wished to visit a fair in County Wicklow, and as the buying and selling in these fairs are got through very early in the morning I started soon after dawn to walk the ten or twelve miles that led to Aughrim, where the fair was to be held. When I came out into the air the cold was intense, though it was a morning of August, and the dew was so heavy that bushes and meadows of mountain grass seemed to have lost their greenness in silvery grey. In the glens I went through white mists were twisting and feathering themselves into extraordinary shapes, and showing blue hills behind them that looked singularly desolate and far away. At every turn I came on multitudes of rabbits feeding on the roadside, or on even shyer creatures — corncrakes, squirrels and snipe — close to villages where no one was awake.

Then the sun rose, and I could see lines of smoke beginning to go up from farm-houses under the hills, and sometimes a sleepy, half-dressed girl looked out of the door of a cottage when my feet echoed on the road. About six miles from Aughrim I began to fall in with droves of bullocks and sheep, in charge of two or three dogs and a herd, or with whole families of mountain people, driving nothing but a single donkey or kid. These people seemed to feel already the animation of the fair, and were talking eagerly and gaily among themselves. I did not hurry, and it was about nine o'clock when I made my way into the village, which was now thronged with cattle and sheep. On every side the usual half-humorous bargaining could be heard above the noise of the pigs and donkeys and lambs. One man would say:

'Are you going to not divide a shilling with me? Are you going to not do it? You're the biggest schemer ever walked down into Aughrim.'

A little further on a man said to a seller: 'You're asking too much for them lambs.' The seller answered: 'If I didn't ask it how would I ever get it? The lambs is good lambs, and if you buy them now you'll get home nice and easy in time to have your dinner in comfort, and if you don't buy them you'll be here the whole day sweating in the heat and dust, and maybe not please yourself in the end of all.'

Then they began looking at the lambs again, talking of the cleanness of their skin and the quality of the wool, and making many extravagant remarks in their praise or against them. As I turned away I heard the loud clap of one hand into another, which always marks the conclusion of a bargain.

A little further on I found a farmer I knew standing before a public-house, looking radiant with delight. 'It's a fine fair, Mister,' he said, 'and I'm after selling the lambs I had here a month ago and no one would look at them. Then I took them to Rathdrum and Wicklow, getting up at three in the morning, and driving them in the creel, and it all for nothing. But I'm shut of them now, and it's not too bad a price

I've got either. I'm after driving the lambs outside the customs (the boundary where the fair tolls are paid), and I'm waiting now for my money.' While we were talking, a cry of warning was raised: 'Mind yourselves below there's a drift of sheep coming down the road.' Then a couple of men and dogs appeared, trying to drive a score of sheep that some one had purchased, out of the village, between the countless flocks that were standing already on either side of the way. This task is peculiarly difficult. Boys and men collect round the flock that is to be driven out, and try to force the animals down the narrow passage that is left in the middle of the road. It hardly ever happens, however, that they get through without carrying off a few of some one else's sheep, or losing some of their own, which have to be restored, or looked for afterwards.

The flock was driven by as well as could be managed, and a moment later an old man came up to us, and asked if we had seen a ewe passing from the west. 'A sheep is after passing,' said the farmer I was talking to, 'but it was not one of yours, for it was too wilful; it was a mountain sheep.' Sometimes animals are astray in this way for a considerable time — it is not unusual to meet a man the day after a fair wandering through the country, asking after a lost heifer, or ewe — but they are always well marked and are found in the end.

When I reached the green above the village I found the curious throng one always meets in these fairs, made up of wild mountain squatters, gentlemen farmers, jobbers and herds. At one corner of the green there was the usual camp of tinkers, where a swarm of children had been left to play among the carts while the men and women wandered through the fair selling cans or donkeys. Many odd types of tramps and beggars had come together also, and were loitering about in the hope of getting some chance job, or of finding some one who would stand them a drink. Once or twice a stir was made by some unruly ram or bull, but in these smaller fairs there seldom is much real excitement till the evening, when the bad whisky that is too freely drunk begins to be felt.

When I had spoken to one or two men that I wished to see, I sat down near a bridge at the end of the green, between a tinker who was mending a can and a herd who was minding some sheep that had not been sold. The herd spoke to me with some pride of his skill in dipping sheep to keep them from the fly, and other matters connected with his work. 'Let you not be talking,' said the tinker, when he paused for a moment. 'You've been after sheep since you were that height' (holding his hand a little over the ground), 'and yet you're nowhere in the world beside the herds that do be reared beyond on the mountains. Those men are a wonder, for I'm told they can tell a lamb from their own ewes before it is marked; and that when they have five hundred sheep on the hills — five hundred is a big number — they don't need to count them or reckon them at all, but they just walk here and there where they are, and if one is gone away they'll miss it from the rest.'

Then a woman came up and spoke to the tinker, and they went down the road together into the village. 'That man is a great villain,' said the herd, when he was out of hearing. 'One time he and his woman went up to a priest in the hills and asked him would he wed them for half a sovereign, I think it was. The priest said it was a poor price, but he'd wed them surely if they'd make him a tin can along with it. "I will, faith," said the tinker, "and I'll come back when it's done." They went off then, and in three weeks they came back, and they asked the priest a second time would he wed them. "Have you the tin can?" said the priest. "We have not," said the tinker; "we had it made at the fall of night, but the ass gave it a kick this morning the way it isn't fit for you at all." "Go on now," says the priest. "It's a pair of rogues and schemers you are, and I won't wed you at all." They went off then, and they were never married to this day.'

As I went up again through the village a great sale of old clothing was going on from booths at each side of the road, and further on boots were set out for sale on boards laid across the tops of barrels, a very usual counter. In another place old women were selling quantities of damaged fruit, kippered herrings, and an extraordinary collection of old ropes and iron. In front of a public-house a ballad-singer was singing a song in the middle of a crowd of people. As far as I could hear it, the words ran like this:

As we came down from Wicklow
With our bundle of switches
As we came down from Wicklow,
Oh! what did we see?
As we came to the city
We saw maidens pretty,

And we called out to ask them to buy our heath-broom.
Heath-broom, freestone, black turf, gather them up.
Oh! gradh machree, Mavourneen,
Won't you buy our heath-broom?
When the season is over
Won't we be in clover,
With the gold in our pockets
We got from heath-broom.

It's home we will toddle,
And we'll get a naggin,
And we'll drink to the maidens that bought our heath-broom.
Heath-broom, freestone, black turf, gather them up.
Oh! gradh machree, Mavourneen,
Won't you buy our heath-broom?

Before he had finished a tinker arrived, too drunk to stand or walk, but leading a tall horse with his left hand, and inviting anyone who would deny that he was the best horseman in Wicklow to fight with him on the spot. Soon afterwards I started on my way home, driving most of the way with a farmer from the same neighbourhood.

A Landlord's Garden in County Wicklow

A STONE'S throw from an old house where I spent several summers in County Wicklow, there was a garden that had been left to itself for fifteen or twenty years. Just inside the gate, as one entered, two paths led up through a couple of strawberry beds, half choked with leaves, where a few white and narrow strawberries were still hidden away. Further on was nearly half an acre of tall raspberry canes and thistles five feet high, growing together in a dense mass, where one could still pick raspberries enough to last a household for the season. Then, in a waste of hemlock, there were some half-dozen apple trees covered with lichen and moss, and against the northern walls a few dying plum trees hanging from their nails. Beyond them there was a dead pear tree, and just inside the gate, as one came back to it, a large fuchsia filled with empty nests. A few lines of box here and there showed where the flower-beds had been laid out, and when anyone who had the knowledge looked carefully among them many remnants could be found of beautiful and rare plants.

All round this garden there was a wall seven or eight feet high, in which one could see three or four tracks with well-worn holes — like the paths down a cliff in Kerry — where boys and tramps came over to steal and take away any apples or other fruits that were in season. Above the wall on the three windy sides there were rows of finely-grown lime trees, the place of meeting in the summer for ten thousand bees. Under the east wall there was the roof of a green-house, where one could sit, when it was wet or dry, and watch the birds and butterflies, many of which were not common. The seasons were always late in this place — it was high above the sea — and redpoles often used to nest not far off late in the summer; siskins did the same once or twice, and greenfinches, till the beginning of August, used to cackle endlessly in the lime trees.

Everyone is used in Ireland to the tragedy that is bound up with the lives of farmers and fishing people; but in this garden one seemed to feel the tragedy of the landlord class also, and of the innumerable old families that are quickly dwindling away. These owners of the land are not much pitied at the present day, or much deserving of pity; and yet one cannot quite forget that they are the descendants of what was at one time, in the eighteenth century, a high-spirited and highly-cultivated aristocracy. The broken greenhouses and mouse-eaten libraries, that were designed and collected by men who voted with Grattan, are perhaps as mournful in the end as the four mud walls that are so often left in Wicklow as the only remnants of a farmhouse. The desolation of this life is often of a peculiarly local kind, and if a playwright chose to go through the Irish country houses he would find material, it is likely, for many gloomy plays that would turn on the dying away of these old families, and on the lives of the one or two delicate girls that are left so often to represent a dozen hearty men who were alive a generation or two ago. Many of the descendants of these people have, of course, drifted into professional life in Dublin, or have gone abroad; yet, wherever they are, they do not equal their forefathers, and where men used to collect fine editions of Don Quixote and Moliere, in Spanish and French, and luxuriantly bound copies of Juvenal and Persius and Cicero, nothing is read now but Longfellow and Hall Caine and Miss Corelli. Where good and roomy houses were built a hundred years ago, poor and tawdry houses are built now; and bad bookbinding, bad pictures, and bad decorations are thought well of, where rich bindings, beautiful miniatures, and finely-carved chimney-pieces were once prized by the old Irish landlords.

To return to our garden. One year the apple crop was unusually plentiful, and every Sunday inroads were made upon it by some unknown persons. At last I decided to lie in wait at the dangerous hour — about twelve o'clock — when the boys of the neighbourhood were on their way home from Mass, and we were supposed to be busy with our devotions three miles away. A little before eleven I slipped out, accordingly, with a book, locked the door behind me, put the key in my pocket, and lay down under a bush. When I had been reading for some time, and had quite forgotten the thieves, I looked up at some little stir and saw a young man, in his Sunday clothes, walking up the path towards me. He stopped when he saw me, and for a moment we gazed at each other with astonishment. At last, to make a move, I said it was a fine day. 'It is indeed, sir,' he answered with a smile, and then he turned round and ran for his life. I realized that he was a thief and jumped up and ran after him, seeing, as I did so, a flock of small boys swarming up the walls of the garden. Meanwhile the young man ran round and round through the raspberry canes, over the strawberry beds, and in and out among the apple trees. He knew that if he tried to get over the wall I should catch him, and that there was no other way out, as I had locked the gate. It was heavy running, and we both began to get weary. Then I caught my foot in a briar and fell. Immediately the young man rushed to the wall and began scrambling up it, but just as he was drawing his leg over the top I caught him by the heel. For a moment he struggled and kicked, then by sheer weight I brought him down at my feet, and an armful of masonry along with him. I caught him by the neck and tried to ask his name, but found we were too breathless to speak.

For I do not know how long we sat glaring at each other, and gasping painfully. Then by degrees I began to upbraid him in a whisper for coming over a person's wall to steal his apples, when he was such a fine, well-dressed, grownup young man. I could see that he was in mortal dread that I might have him up in the police courts, which I had no intention of doing, and when I finally asked him his name and address he invented a long story of how he lived six miles away, and had come over to this neighbourhood for Mass and to see a friend, and then how he had got a drought upon him, and thought an apple would put him in spirits for his walk home. Then he swore he would never come over the wall again if I would let him off, and that he would pray God to have mercy on me when my last hour was come. I felt sure his whole story was a tissue of lies, and I did not want him to have the crow of having taken me in. 'There is a woman belonging to the place,' I said, 'inside in the house helping the girl to cook the dinner. Walk in now with me, and we'll see if you're such a stranger as you'd have me think.' He looked infinitely troubled, but I took him by the neck and wrist and we set off for the gate. When we had gone a pace or two he stopped. 'I beg your pardon,' he said, 'my cap's after falling down on the over side of the wall. May I cross over and get it?' That was too much for me. 'Well, go on,' I said, 'and if ever I catch you again woe betide you.' I let him go then, and he rushed madly over the wall and disappeared. A few days later I discovered, not at all to my surprise, that he lived half a mile away, and was intimately related to a small boy who came to the house every morning to run messages and clean the boots. Yet it must not be thought that this young man was dishonest; I would have been quite ready the next day to trust him with a ten-pound note.

Glencree

THIS morning the air is clear, and there is a trace of summer again. I am sitting in a nook beside the stream from the Upper Lake, close down among the heather and bracken and rushes. I have seen the people going up to Mass in the Reformatory, and the valley seems empty of life.

I have gone on, mile after mile, of the road to Sally Gap, between brown dykes and chasms in the turf with broken foot-bridges across them, or between sheets of sickly moss and bog-cotton that is unable to thrive. The road is caked with moss that breaks like pie-crust under my feet, and in corners where there is shelter there are sheep loitering, or a few straggling grouse.... The fog has come down in places; I am meeting multitudes of hares that run round me at a little distance — looking enormous in the mists — or sit up on their ends against the sky line to watch me going by. When I sit down for a moment the sense of loneliness has no equal. I can hear nothing but the slow running of water and the grouse crowing and chuckling underneath the band of cloud. Then the fog lifts and shows the white empty roads winding everywhere, with the added sense of desolation one gets passing an empty house on the side of a road.

When I turn back again the air has got stuffy and heavy and calm, with a cloud still down upon the glen; there is a dead heat in the air that is not natural so high up, and the silence is so great three or four wrens that are singing near the lake seem to fill the valley with sound. In most places I can see the straight ending of the cloud, but above the lake grey fingers are coming up and down, like a hand that is clasping and opening again. One longs for rain or wind or thunder. The very ewes and lambs have stopped bleating, and are slinking round among the stacks of turf.

I have come out again on the mountain road the third day of the fog. At first it was misty only, and then a cloud crept up the water gullies from the valley of the Liffey, and in a moment I am cut off in a white silent cloud. The little turfy ridges on each side of the road have the look of glens to me, and every block of stone has the size of a house. The cobwebs on the furze are like a silvery net, and the silence is so great and queer, even weazels run squealing past me on the side of the road.... An east wind is rising. Once in every minute I see the little mounds in their natural shapes that have been mountains for a week. I see wet cottages on the other side of the glen that I had forgotten. Then, as I walk on, I see out over a cloud to the tops of real mountains standing up into the sky.

There is a dense white fog around the cottage, and we seem to be shut away from any habitation. All round behind the hills there is a moan and rumble of thunder coming nearer, at times with a fierce and sudden crash. The bracken has a nearly painful green in the strangeness of the light. Enormous sheep are passing in and out of the sky line.

There is a strange depression about the cottage to-night. The woman of the house is taken ill and has got into bed beside her mother-in-law, who is over ninety, and is wandering in her mind. The man of the house has gone away ten miles for medicine, and I am left with the two children, who are playing silently about the door.

The larches in the haggard are dripping heavily with damp, and the hens and geese, bewildered with the noise and gloom, are cackling with uneasy dread. All one's senses are disturbed. As I walk backwards and forwards, a few yards above and below the door, the little stream I do not see seems to roar out of the cloud.

Every leaf and twig is heavy with drops, and a dog that has passed with a sad-eyed herd looked wet and draggled and afraid.

I remember lying in the heather one clear Sunday morning in the early autumn when the bracken had just turned. All the people of the district were at Mass in a chapel a few miles away, so the valleys were empty, and there was nothing to be heard but the buzzing of a few late bees and the autumn song of thrushes. The sky was covered with white radiant clouds, with soft outlines, broken in a few places by lines of blue sky of wonderful delicacy and clearness. In a little while I heard a step on a path beneath me, and a tramp came wandering round the bottom of the hill. There was a spring below where I was lying, and when he reached it he looked round to see if anyone was watching him. I was hidden by the ferns, so he knelt down beside the water, where there was a pool among the stones, pulled his shirt over his head, and began washing it in the spring. After a little he seemed satisfied, and began wringing the water out of it; then he put it on, dripping as it was, buttoned his old coat over it, and wandered on towards the village, picking blackberries from the hedge.

In West Kerry

AT Tralee station — I was on my way to a village many miles beyond Dingle — I found a boy who carried my bag some way along the road to an open yard, where the light railway starts for the west. There was a confused mass of peasants struggling on the platform, with all sort of baggage, which the people lifted into the train for themselves as well as they were able. The seats ran up either side of the cars, and the space between them was soon filled with sacks of flour, cases of porter, chairs rolled in straw, and other household goods. A drunken young man got in just before we started, and sang songs for a few coppers, telling us that he had spent all his money, and had nothing left to pay for his ticket. Then, when the carriage was closely packed, we moved slowly out of the station. At my side there was an old man who explained the Irish names of the places that we came to, and pointed out the Seven Pigs, a group of islands in the bay; Kerry Head, further off; and many distant mountains. Beyond him a dozen big women in shawls were crowded together; and just opposite me there was a young woman wearing a wedding ring, who was one of the peculiarly refined women of Kerry, with supreme charm in every movement and expression. The big woman talked to her about some elderly man who had been sick — her husband, it was likely — and some young man who had gone away to England, and was breaking his heart with loneliness.

'Ah, poor fellow!' she said; 'I suppose he will get used to it like another; and wouldn't he be worse off if he was beyond the seas in Saint Louis, or the towns of America?'

This woman seemed to unite the healthiness of the country people with the greatest sensitiveness, and whenever there was any little stir or joke in the carriage, her face and neck flushed with pleasure and amusement. As we went on there were superb sights — first on the north, towards Loop Head, and then when we reached the top of the ridge, to the south also, to Drung Hill, Macgillicuddy's Reeks, and other mountains of South Kerry. A little further on, nearly all the people got out at a small station; and the young woman I had admired gathered up most of the household goods and got down also, lifting heavy boxes with the power of a man. Then two returned American girls got in, fine, stout-looking women, with distress in their expression, and we started again. Dingle Bay could now be seen through narrow valleys on our left, and had extraordinary beauty in the evening light. In the carriage next to ours a number of herds and jobbers were travelling, and for the last hour they kept up a furious altercation that seemed always on the verge of breaking out into a dangerous quarrel, but no blows were given.

At the end of the line an old blue side-car was waiting to take me to the village where I was going. I was some time fastening on my goods, with the raggedy boy who was to drive me; and then we set off passing through the usual streets of a Kerry town, with public-houses at the corners, till we left the town by a narrow quay with a few sailing boats and a small steamer with coal. Then we went over a bridge near a large water-mill, where a number of girls were standing about, with black shawls over their heads, and turned sharp to the right, against the face of the mountains. At first we went up hill for several miles, and got on slowly, though the boy jumped down once or twice and gathered a handful of switches to beat the tall mare he was driving. Just as the twilight was beginning to deepen we reached the top of the ridge and came out through a gap into sight of Smerwick Harbour, a wild bay with magnificent headlands beyond it, and a long stretch of the Atlantic. We drove on towards the west, sometimes very quickly, where the slope was gradual, and then slowly again when the road seemed to fall away under us, like the wall of a house. As the night fell the sea became like a piece of white silver on our right; and the mountains got black on our left, and heavy night smells began to come up out of the bogs. Once or twice I noticed a blue cloud over the edge of the road, and then I saw that we were nearly against the gables of a little village, where the houses were so closely packed together there was no light from any of them. It was now quite dark, and the boy got cautious in his driving, pulling the car almost into the ditch once or twice to avoid an enormous cavity where the middle of the road had settled down into the bogs. At last we came to another river and a public-house, and went up a hill, from which we could see the outline of a chapel; then the boy turned to me: 'Is it ten o'clock yet?' he said; 'for we're mostly now in the village.'

This morning, a Sunday, rain was threatening; but I went out west after my breakfast under Croagh

Martin, in the direction of the Atlantic. At one of the first villages I came to I had a long talk with a man who was sitting on the ditch waiting till it was time for Mass. Before long we began talking about the Irish language.

'A few years ago,' he said, 'they were all for stopping it off; and when I was a boy they tied a gobban into my mouth for the whole afternoon because I was heard speaking Irish. Wasn't that great cruelty? And now when I hear the same busybodies coming around and telling us for the love of God to speak nothing but Irish, I've a good mind to tell them to go to hell. There was a priest out here a while since who was telling us to stay always where we are, and to speak nothing but Irish; but, I suppose, although the priests are learned men, and great scholars, they don't understand the life of the people the same as another man would. In this place the land is poor — you can see that for yourself — and the people have little else to live on; so that when there is a long family, one son will stay at home and keep on the farm, and the others will go away because they must go. Then when they once pass out of the Dingle station in Tralee they won't hear a word of Irish, or meet anyone who'd understand it; so what good, I ask you, is a man who hasn't got the English, and plenty of it?'

After I left him I went on towards Dunquin, and lay for a long time on the side of a magnificently wild road under Croagh Martin, where I could see the Blasket Islands and the end of Dunmore Head, the most westerly point of Europe. It was a grey day, with a curious silence on the sea and sky and no sign of life anywhere, except the sail of one curagh — or niavogue, as they are called here — that was sailing in from the islands. Now and then a cart passed me filled with old people and children, who saluted me in Irish; then I turned back myself. I got on a long road running through a bog, with a smooth mountain on one side and the sea on the other, and Brandon in front of me, partly covered with clouds. As far as I could see there were little groups of people on their way to the chapel in Ballyferriter, the men in homespun and the women wearing blue cloaks, or, more often, black shawls twisted over their heads. This procession along the olive bogs, between the mountains and the sea, on this grey day of autumn, seemed to wring me with the pang of emotion one meets everywhere in Ireland — an emotion that is partly local and patriotic, and partly a share of the desolation that is mixed everywhere with the supreme beauty of the world.

In the evening, when I was walking about the village, I fell in with a man who could read Gaelic, and was full of enthusiasm for the old language and of contempt for English.

'I can tell you,' he said, 'that the English I have is no more good to me than the cover of that pipe. Buyers come here from Dingle and Cork and Clare, and they have good Irish, and so has everyone we meet with, for there is no one can do business in this place who hasn't the language on his tongue.'

Then I asked him about the young men who go away to America.

'Many go away,' he said, 'who could stay if they

wished to, for it is a fine place for fishing, and a man will get more money and better health for himself, and rear a better family, in this place than in many another. It's a good place to be in, and now, with the help of God, the little children will all learn to read and write in Irish, and that is a great thing, for how can people do any good, or make a song even, if they cannot write? You will be often three weeks making a song, and there will be times when you will think of good things to put into it that could never be beaten in the whole world; but if you cannot write them down you will forget them, maybe, by the next day, and then what good will be your song?'

After a while we went upstairs to a large room in the inn, where a number of young men and girls were dancing jigs and reels. These young people, although they are as Irish-speaking as the people of Connemara, are pushing forward in their ways of living and dress; so that this group of dancers could hardly have been known, by their appearance, from any Sunday party in Limerick or Cork. After a long four-hand reel, my friend, who was dressed in homespun, danced a jig to the whistling of a young man with great energy and spirit. Then he sat down beside me in the corner, and we talked about spring trawling and the price of nets. I told him about the ways of Aran and Connemara; and then he told me about the French trawlers who come to this neighbourhood in April and May.

'The Frenchmen from Fecamp,' he said, 'are Catholics and decent people; but those who come from Boulogne have no religion, and are little better than a wild beast would lep on you out of a wood.

One night there was a drift of them below in the public-house, where there is a counter, as you've maybe seen, with a tin top on it. Well, they were talking together, and they had some little difference among themselves, and from that they went on raising their voices, till one of them out with his knife and drove it down through the tin into the wood! Wasn't that a dangerous fellow?'

Then he told me about their tobacco.

'The French do have two kinds of tobacco; one of them is called hay-tobacco, and if you give them a few eggs, or maybe nine little cabbage plants, they'll give you as much of it as would fill your hat. Then we get a pound of our own tobacco and mix the two of them together, and put them away in a pig's bladder — it's that way we keep our tobacco — and we have enough with that lot for the whole winter.'

This evening a circus was advertised in Dingle, for one night only; so I made my way there towards the end of the afternoon, although the weather was windy and threatening. I reached the town an hour too soon, so I spent some time watching the wild-looking fishermen and fish-women who stand about the quays. Then I wandered up and saw the evening train coming in with the usual number of gaily-dressed young women and half-drunken jobbers and merchants; and at last, about eight o'clock, I went to the circus field, just above the town, in a heavy splash of rain. The tent was set up in the middle of the field, and a little to the side of it a large crowd was struggling for tickets at one of the wheeled houses in which the acrobats live. I went round the tent in the hope of getting in by some easier means, and found a door in the canvas, where a man was calling out: 'Tickets, or money, this way,' and I passed in through a long winding passage. It was some time after the hour named for the show, but although the tent was almost filled there was no sign of the performers; so I stood back in a corner and watched the crowd coming in wet and dripping from the rain, which had turned to a downpour. The tent was lighted by a few flaring gas-jets round the central pole, with an opening above them, through which the rain shot down in straight whistling lines. The top of the tent was dripping and saturated, and the gas, shining sideways across, made it glitter in many places with the brilliancy of golden silk. When a sudden squall came with a rush from the narrow valleys behind the town, the whole structure billowed, and flapped and strained, till one waited every moment to see the canvas fall upon our heads. The people, who looked strangely black and swarthy in the uncertain light, were seated all round on three or four rows of raised wooden seats, and many who were late were still crushing forward, and standing in dense masses wherever there was room. At the entrance a rather riotous crowd began to surge in so quickly that there was some danger of the place being rushed. Word was sent across the ring, and in a moment three or four of the women performers, with long streaming ulsters buttoned over their tights, ran out from behind the scenes and threw themselves into the crowd, forcing back the wild hill-side people, fishwomen and drunken sailors, in an extraordinary tumult of swearing, wrestling and laughter. These women seemed to enjoy this part of their work, and shrieked with amusement when two or three of them fell on some enormous farmer or publican and nearly dragged him to the ground. Here and there among the people I could see a little party of squireens and their daughters, in the fashions of five years ago, trying, not always successfully, to reach the shilling seats. The crowd was now so thick I could see little more than the heads of the performers, who had at last come into the ring, and many of the shorter women who were near me must have seen nothing the whole evening, yet they showed no sign of impatience. The performance was begun by the usual dirty white horse, that was brought out and set to gallop round, with a gaudy horse-woman on his back, who jumped through a hoop and did the ordinary feats, the horse's hoofs splashing and possing all the time in the green slush of the ring. An old door-mat was laid down near the entrance for the performers, and as they came out in turn they wiped the mud from their feet before they got up on their horses. A little later the clown came out, to the great delight of the people. He was followed by some gymnasts, and then the horse-people came out again in different dress and make-up, and went through their old turns once more. After that there was prolonged fooling between the clown and the chief horseman, who made many mediaeval jokes, that reminded me of little circuses on the outer boulevards of Paris, and at last the horseman sang a song which won great applause:

Here's to the man who kisses his wife,
And kisses his wife alone;
For there's many a man kissed another man's wife

When he thought he kissed his own.
Here's to the man who rocks his child,
And rocks his child alone;
For there's many a man rocked another man's child
When he thought he rocked his own.

About ten o'clock there seemed to be a lull in the storm, so I went out into the open air with two young men who were going the road I had to travel. The rain had stopped for a moment, but a high wind was blowing as we made our way to a public-house to get a few biscuits and a glass of beer before we started. A sleepy barmaid, who was lolling behind the counter with a novel, pricked up her ears when she heard us talking of our journey.

'Surely you are not going to Ballydavid,' she said, 'at such an hour of a night like this.'

We told her we were going to a place which was further away.

'Well,' she said, 'I wouldn't go to that place to-night if you had a coach-and-four to drive me in, and gave me twenty pounds into the bargain! How at all will you get on in the darkness when the roads will be running with water, and you'll be likely to slip down every place into some drain or ditch?'

When we went out, and began to make our way down the steep hill through the town, the night seemed darker than ever after the glare of the bar. Before we had gone many yards a woman's voice called out sharply from under the wall: 'Mind the horse.' I looked up and saw the black outline of a horse's head standing right above me. It was not plain in such darkness how we should get to the end of our ten-mile journey; but one of the young men borrowed a lantern from a chandler in the bottom of the town, and we made our way over the bridge and up the hill, going slowly and painfully with just light enough, when we kept close together, to avoid the sloughs of water and piles of stones on the roadway. By the time we reached the top of the ridge and began to work down carefully towards Smerwick, the rain stopped, and we reached the village without any mishap.

I go out often in the mornings to the site of Sybil Ferriter's Castle, on a little headland reached by a narrow strip of rocks. As I lie there I can watch whole flights of cormorants and choughs and seagulls that fly about under the cliffs, and beyond them a number of niavogues that are nearly always fishing in Ferriter's Cove. Further on there are Sybil Head and three rocky points, the Three Sisters then Smerwick Harbour and Brandon far away, usually covered with white airy clouds. Between these headlands and the village there is a strip of sandhill grown over with sea-holly, and a low beach where scores of red bullocks lie close to the sea, or wade in above their knees. Further on one passes peculiar horseshoe coves, with contorted lines of sandstone on one side and slaty blue rocks on the other, and necks of transparent sea of wonderful blueness between them.

I walked up this morning along the slope from the east to the top of Sybil Head, where one comes out suddenly on the brow of a cliff with a straight fall of many hundred feet into the sea. It is a place of indescribable grandeur, where one can see Carrantuohill and the Skelligs and Loop Head and the full sweep of the Atlantic, and, over all, the wonderfully tender and searching light that is seen only in Kerry. Looking down the drop of five or six hundred feet, the height is so great that the gannets flying close over the sea look like white butterflies, and the choughs like flies fluttering behind them. One wonders in these places why anyone is left in Dublin, or London, or Paris, when it would be better, one would think, to live in a tent or hut with this magnificent sea and sky, and to breathe this wonderful air, which is like wine in one's teeth.

Here and there on this headland there are little villages of ten or twenty houses, closely packed together without any order or roadway. Usually there are one or two curious beehive-like structures in these villages, used here, it is said, as pigsties or storehouses. On my way down from Sybil Head I was joined by a tall young man, who told me he had been in the navy, but had bought himself out before his time was over. 'Twelve of us joined from this place,' he said, 'and I was the last of them that stayed in it, for it is a life that no one could put up with. It's not the work that would trouble you, but it's that they can't leave you alone, and that you must be ever and always fooling over something.'

He had been in South Africa during the war, and in Japan, and all over the world; but he was now dressed in homespuns, and had settled down here, he told me, for the rest of his life. Before we reached the village we met Maurice, the fisherman I have spoken of and we sat down under a hedge to shelter from a shower. We began to talk of fevers and sicknesses and doctors — these little villages are often infested with typhus — and Maurice spoke about the traditional cures.

'There is a plant,' he said, 'which is the richest that is growing out of the ground, and in the old times the women used to be giving it to their children till they'd be growing up seven feet maybe in height. Then the priests and doctors began taking everything to themselves and destroyed the old knowledge, and that is a poor thing; for you know well it was the Holy Mother of God who cured her own Son with plants the like of that, and said after that no mother should be without a plant for ever to cure her child. Then she threw out the seeds of it over the whole world, so that it's growing every place from that day to this.'

I came out to-day, a holiday, to the Great Blasket Island with a schoolmaster and two young men from the village, who were coming for the afternoon only. The day was admirably clear, with a blue sea and sky, and the voyage in the long canoe — I had not been in one for two or three years — gave me indescribable enjoyment. We passed Dunmore Head, and then stood Out nearly due west towards the Great Blasket itself, the height of the mountains round the bay and the sharpness of the rocks making the place singularly different from the sounds about Aran, where I had last travelled in a curagh. As usual, three men were rowing — the man I have come to stay with, his son, and a tall neighbour, all dressed in blue jerseys, homespun trousers and shirts, and talking in Irish only, though my host could speak good English when he chose to. As we came nearer the island, which seemed to rise like a mountain straight out of the sea, we could make out a crowd of people in their holiday clothes standing or sitting along the brow of the cliff watching our approach, and just beyond them a patch of cottages with roofs of tarred felt. A little later we doubled into a cove among the rocks, where I landed at a boat slip, and then scrambled up a steep zig-zag pathway to the head of the cliff where the people crowded round us and shook hands with the men who had come with me.

This cottage where I am to stay is one of the highest of the group, and as we passed up to it through little paths among the cottages many white, wolfish-looking dogs came out and barked furiously. My host had gone on in front with my bag, and when I reached his threshold he came forward and shook hands with me again, with a finished speech of welcome. His eldest daughter, a young married woman of about twenty, who manages the house, shook hands with me also, and then, without asking if we were hungry, began making us tea in a metal teapot and frying rashers of bacon. She is a small, beautifully-formed woman, with brown hair and eyes — instead of the black hair and blue eyes that are usually found with this type in Ireland — and delicate feet and ankles that are not common in these parts, where the woman's work is so hard. Her sister, who lives in the house also, is a bonny girl of about eighteen, full of humour and spirits.

The schoolmaster made many jokes in English and Irish while the little hostess served our tea and then the kitchen filled up with young men and women — the men dressed like ordinary fishermen, the women wearing print bodices and coloured skirts, that had none of the distinction of the dress of Aran — and a polka was danced, with curious solemnity, in a whirl of dust. When it was over it was time for my companions to go back to the mainland. As soon as we came out and began to go down to the sea, a large crowd, made up of nearly all the men and women and children of the island, came down also, closely packed round us. At the edge of the cliff the young men and the schoolmaster bade me good-bye and went down the zig-zag path, leaving me alone with the islanders on the ledge of rock, where I had seen the people as we came in. I sat for a long time watching the sail of the canoe moving away to Dunquin, and talking to a young man who had spent some years in Ballyferriter, and had good English. The evening was peculiarly fine, and after a while, when the crowd had scattered, I passed up through the cottages, and walked through a boreen towards the north-west, between a few plots of potatoes and little fields of weeds that seemed to have gone out of cultivation not long ago. Beyond these I turned up a sharp, green hill, and came out suddenly on the broken edge of a cliff. The effect was wonderful. The Atlantic was right underneath; then I could see the sharp rocks of several uninhabited islands, a mile or two off, the Tearaught further away, and, on my left, the whole northern edge of this island curving round towards the west, with a steep heathery face, a thousand feet high. The whole sight of wild islands and sea was as clear and cold and brilliant as what one sees in a dream, and alive with the singularly severe glory that is in the character of this place.

As I was wandering about I saw many of the younger islanders not far off jumping and putting the weight — a heavy stone — or running races on the grass. Then four girls, walking arm-in-arm, came up and talked to me in Irish. Before long they began to laugh loudly at some signs I made to eke out my meaning, and by degrees the men wandered up also, till there was a crowd round us. The cold of the night was growing stronger, however, and we soon turned back to the village, and sat round the fire in the kitchen the rest of the evening.

At eleven o'clock the people got up as one man and went away, leaving me with the little hostess — the man of the house had gone to the mainland with the young men — her husband and sister. I told them I was sleepy, and ready to go to bed; so the little hostess lighted a candle, carried it into the room beyond the kitchen, and stuck it up on the end of the bedpost of one of the beds with a few drops of grease. Then she took off her apron, and fastened it up in the window as a blind, laid another apron on the wet earthen floor for me to stand on, and left me to myself. The room had two beds, running from wall to wall with a small space between them, a chair that the little hostess had brought in, an old hair-brush that was propping the window open, and no other article. When I had been in bed for some time, I heard the host's voice in the kitchen, and a moment or two later he came in with a candle in his hand, and made a long apology for having been away the whole of my first evening on the island, holding the candle while he talked very close to my face. I told him I had been well entertained by his family and neighbours, and had hardly missed him. He went away, and half an hour later opened the door again with the iron spoon which serves to lift the latch, and came in, in a suit of white homespuns, and said he must ask me to let him stretch out in the other bed, as there was no place else for him to lie. I told him that he was welcome, and he got into the other bed and lit his pipe. Then we had a long talk about this place and America and the younger generations.

'There has been no one drowned on this island,' he said, 'for forty years, and that is a great wonder, for it is a dangerous life. There was a man — the brother of the man you were talking to when the girls were dancing — was married to a widow had a public-house away to the west of Ballydavid, and he was out fishing for mackerel, and he got a great haul of them; then he filled his canoe too full, so that she was down to the edge in the water, and a wave broke into her when they were near the shore, and she went down under them. Two men got ashore, but the man from this island was drowned, for his oilskins went down about his feet, and he sank where he was.'

Then we talked about the chances of the mackerel season. 'If the season is good,' he said, 'we get on well; but it is not certain at all. We do pay four pounds for a net, and sometimes the dogfish will get into it the first day and tear it into pieces as if you'd cut it with a knife. Sometimes the mackerel will die in the net, and then ten men would be hard set to pull them up into the canoe, so that if the wind rises on us we must cut loose, and let down the net to the bottom of the sea. When we get fish here in the night we go to Dunquin and sell them to buyers in the morning; and, believe me, it is a dangerous thing to cross that sound when you have too great a load taken into your canoe. When it is too bad to cross over we do salt the fish ourselves — we must salt them cleanly and put them in clean barrels — and then the first day it is calm buyers will be out after them from the town of Dingle.'

Afterwards he spoke of the people who go away to America, and the younger generations that are growing up now in Ireland.

'The young people is no use,' he said. 'I am not as good a man as my father was, and my son is growing up worse than I am.' Then he put up his pipe on the end of the bed-post. 'You'll be tired now,' he went on, 'so it's time we were sleeping; and, I humbly beg your pardon, might I ask your name?' I told him.

'Well, good night so,' he said, 'and may you have a good sleep your first night in this island.'

Then he put out the candle and we settled to sleep. In a few minutes I could hear that he was in his dreams, and just as my own ideas were beginning to wander the house door opened, and the son of the place, a young man of about twenty, came in and walked into our room, close to my bed, with another candle in his hand. I lay with my eyes closed, and the young man did not seem pleased with my presence, though he looked at me with curiosity. When he was satisfied he went back to the kitchen and took a drink of whisky and said his prayers; then, after loitering about for some time and playing with a little mongrel greyhound that seemed to adore him, he took off his clothes, clambered over his father, and stretched out on the inner side of the bed.

I awoke in the morning about six o'clock, and not long afterwards the host awoke also, and asked how I did. Then he wanted to know if I ever drank whisky; and when he heard that I did so, he began calling for one of his daughters at the top of his voice. In a few moments the younger girl came in, her eyes closing with sleep, and, at the host's bidding, got the whisky bottle, some water, and a green wine-glass out of the kitchen. She came first to my bedside and gave me a dram, then she did the same for her father and brother, handed us our pipes and tobacco, and went back to the kitchen.

There were to be sports at noon in Ballyferriter, and when we had talked for a while I asked the host if he would think well of my going over to see them. 'I would not,' he said 'you'd do better to stay quiet in this place where you are; the men will be all drunk coming back, fighting and kicking in the canoes, and a man the like of you, who aren't used to us, would be frightened. Then, if you went, the people would be taking you into one public-house, and then into another, till you'd maybe get drunk yourself, and that wouldn't be a nice thing for a gentleman. Stay where you are in this island and you'll be safest so.'

When the son got up later and began going in

and out of the kitchen, some of the neighbours, who had already come in, stared at me with curiosity as I lay in my bed; then I got up myself and went into the kitchen. The little hostess set about getting my breakfast, but before it was ready she partly rinsed the dough out of a pan where she had been kneading bread, poured some water into it, and put it on a chair near the door. Then she hunted about the edges of the rafters till she found a piece of soap, which she put on the back of a chair with the towel, and told me I might wash my face. I did so as well as I was able, in the middle of the people, and dried myself with the towel, which was the one used by the whole family.

The morning looked as if it would turn to rain and wind, so I took the advice I had been given and let the canoes go off without me to the sports. After a turn on the cliffs I came back to the house to write letters. The little hostess was washing up the breakfast things when I arrived with my papers and pens, but she made room for me at the table, and spread out an old newspaper for me to write on. A little later, when she had finished her washing, she came over to her usual place in the chimney corner, not far from where I was sitting, sat *down* on the floor, and took out her hairpins and began combing her hair. As I finished each letter I had to say who it was to, and where the people lived; and then I had to tell her if they were married or single, how many children they had, and make a guess at how many pounds they spent in the year, and at the number of their servants. Just before I finished, I the younger girl came back with three or four other young women, who were followed in a little while by a party of men.

I showed them some photographs of the Aran Islands and Wicklow, which they looked at with eagerness. The little hostess was especially taken with two or three that had babies or children in their foreground; and as she put her hands on my shoulders, and leaned over to look at them, with the confidence that is so usual in these places, I could see that she had her full share of the passion for children which is powerful in all women who are permanently and profoundly attractive. While I was telling her what I could about the children, I saw one of the men looking with peculiar amazement at an old photograph of myself that had been taken many years ago in an alley of the Luxembourg Gardens, where there were many statues in the background. 'Look at that,' he whispered in Irish to one of the girls, pointing to the statues; 'in those countries they do have naked people standing about in their skins.'

I explained that the figures were of marble only, and then the little hostess and all the girls examined them also. 'Oh! dear me,' said the little hostess, 'Is deas an rud do bheith ag siubhal ins an domhain mor' ('It's a fine thing to be travelling in the big world').

In the afternoon I went up and walked along the narrow central ridge of the island, till I came to the highest point, which is nearly three miles west of the village. The weather was gloomy and wild, and there was something nearly appalling in the loneliness of the place. I could look down on either side into a foggy edge of grey moving sea, and then further off I could see many distant mountains, or look out across the shadowy outline of Inishtooskert to the Tearaught rock. While I was sitting on the little mound which marks the summit of the island — a mound stripped and riddled by rabbits — a heavy bank of fog began to work up from the south, behind Valentia, on the other jaw of Dingle Bay. As soon as I saw it I hurried down from the pinnacle where I was, so that I might get away from the more dangerous locality before the clouds overtook me. In spite of my haste I had not gone half a mile when an edge of fog whisked and circled round me, and in a moment I could see nothing but a grey shroud of mist and a few yards of steep, slippery grass. Everything was distorted and magnified to an extraordinary degree; but I could hear the moan of the sea under me, and I knew my direction, so I worked along towards the village without trouble. In some places the island, on this southern side, is bitten into by sharp, narrow coves, and when the fog opened a little I could see across them, where gulls and choughs were picking about on the grass, looking as big as Kerry cattle or black mountain sheep. Before I reached the house the cloud had turned to a sharp shower of rain, and as I went in the water was dripping from my hat. 'Oh! dear me,' said the little hostess, when she saw me, 'Ta tu an-rhluc anois' ('You are very wet now '). She was alone in the house, breathing audibly with a sort of simple self-importance, as she washed her jugs and teacups. While I was drinking my tea a little later, some woman came in with three or four little girls — the most beautiful children I have ever seen — who live in one of the nearest cottages. They tried to get the little girls to dance a reel together, but the smallest of them went and hid her head in the skirts of the little hostess. In the end two of the little girls danced with two of those who were grown up, to the lilting of one of them. The little hostess sat at the fire while they danced, plucking and drawing a cormorant for the men's dinner, and calling out to the girls when they lost the step of the dance.

In the evenings of Sundays and holidays the young men and girls go out to a rocky headland on the north-west, where there is a long, grassy slope, to dance and amuse themselves; and this evening I wandered out there with two men, telling them ghost stories in Irish as we went. When we turned over the edge of the hill we came on a number of young men lying on the short grass playing cards. We sat down near them, and before long a party of girls and young women came up also and sat down, twenty paces off on the brink of the cliff some of them wearing the fawn-coloured shawls that are so attractive and so much thought of in the south. It was just after sunset, and Inishtooskert was standing out with a smoky blue outline against the redness of the sky. At the foot of the cliff a wonderful silvery light was shining on the sea, which already, before the beginning of autumn, was eager and wintry and cold. The little group of blue-coated men lying on the grass, and the group of girls further off had a singular effect in this solitude of rocks and sea; and in spite of their high spirits it gave me a sort of grief to feel the utter loneliness and desolation of the place that has given these people their finest qualities.

One of the young men had been thrown from a car a few days before on his way home from Dingle, and his face was still raw and bleeding and horrible to look at; but the young girls seemed to find romance in his condition, and several of them went over and sat in a group round him, stroking his arms and face. When the card-playing was over I showed the young men a few tricks and feats, which they worked at themselves, to the great amusement of the girls, till they had accomplished them all. On our way back to the village the young girls ran wild in the twilight, flying and shrieking over the grass, or rushing up behind the young men and throwing them over, if they were able, by a sudden jerk or trip. The men in return caught them by one hand, and spun them round and round four or five times, and then let them go, when they whirled down the grassy slope for many yards, spinning like peg-tops, and only keeping their feet by the greatest efforts or good-luck.

When we got to the village the people scattered for supper, and in our cottage the little hostess swept the floor and sprinkled it with some sand she had brought home in her apron. Then she filled a crock with drinking water, lit the lamp and sat down by the fire to comb her hair. Some time afterwards, when a number of young men had come in, as was usual, to spend the evening, some one said a nia-vogue was on its way home from the sports. We went out to the door, but it was too dark to see anything except the lights of a little steamer that was passing up the sound, almost beneath us, on its way to Limerick or Tralee. When it had gone by we could hear a furious drunken uproar coming up from a canoe that was somewhere out in the bay. It sounded as if the men were strangling or murdering each other, and it seemed almost miraculous that they should be able to manage their canoe. The people seemed to think they were in no special danger, and we went in again to the fire and talked about porter and whisky (I have never heard the men here talk for half an hour of anything without some allusion to drink), discussing how much a man could drink with comfort in a day, whether it is better to drink when a man is thirsty or at ordinary times, and what food gives the best liking for porter. Then they asked me how much porter I could drink myself and I told them I could drink whisky, but that I had no taste for porter, and would only take a pint or two at odd times, when I was thirsty.

'The girls are laughing to hear you say that,' said an old man; 'but whisky is a lighter drink, and I'd sooner have it myself, and any old man would say the same.' A little later some young men came in, in their Sunday clothes, and told us the news of the sports.

This morning it was raining heavily, and the host got out some nets and set to work with his son and son-in-law, mending many holes that had been cut by dog-fish, as the mackerel season is soon to begin. While they were at work the kitchen emptied and filled continually with islanders passing in and out, and discussing the weather and the season. Then they started cutting each other's hair, the man who was being cut sitting with an oilskin round him on a little stool by the door, and some other men came in to sharpen their razors on the host's razor-strop, which seems to be the only one on the island. I had not shaved since I arrived, so the little hostess asked me after a while if I would like to shave myself before dinner. I told her I would, so she got me some water in the potato-dish and put it on a chair; then her sister got me a little piece of broken looking-glass and put it on a nail near the door, where there was some light. I set to work, and as I stood with my back to the people I could catch a score of eyes in the glass, watching me intently. 'That is a great improvement to you now,' said the host, when I had done; 'and whenever you want a beard, God bless you, you'll have a thick one surely.'

When I was coming down in the evening from the ridge of the island, where I spent much of my time looking at the richness of the Atlantic on one side and the sad or shining greys of Dingle Bay on the other, I was joined by two young women and we walked back together. Just outside the village we met an old women who stopped and laughed at us. 'Well, aren't you in good fortune this night, stranger,' she said, 'to be walking up and down in the company of women?'

'I am surely,' I answered; 'isn't that the best thing to be doing in the whole world?'

At our own door I saw the little hostess sweeping the floor, so I went down for a moment to the gable of the cottage, and looked out over the roofs of the little village to the sound, where the tide was running with extraordinary force. In a few minutes the little hostess came down and stood beside me —

she thought I should not be left by myself when I had been driven away by the dust — and I asked her many questions about the names and relationships of the people that I am beginning to know.

Afterwards, when many of the people had come together in the kitchen, the men told me about their lobster-pots that are brought from Southampton, and cost half-a-crown each. 'In good weather,' said the man who was talking to me, 'they will often last for a quarter; but if storms come up on them they will sometimes break up in a week or two. Still and all, it's a good trade; and we do sell lobsters and crayfish every week in the season to a boat from England or a boat from France that does come in here, as you'll maybe see before you go.'

I told them that I had often been in France, and one of the boys began counting up the numerals in French to show what he had learnt from their buyers. A little later, when the talk was beginning to flag, I turned to a young man near me — the best fiddler, I was told, on the island — and asked him to play us a dance. He made excuses, and would not get his fiddle; but two of the girls slipped off and brought it. The young man tuned it and offered it to me, but I insisted that he should take it first. Then he played one or two tunes, without tone, but with good intonation and rhythm. When it was my turn I played a few tunes also; but the pitch was so low I could not do what I wanted, and I had not much success with the people, though the fiddler himself watched me with interest. 'That is great playing,' he said, when I had finished; and I never seen anyone the like of you for moving your hand and getting the sound out of it with the full drag of the bow.' Then he played a polka and four couples danced. The women, as usual, were in their naked feet, and whenever there was a figure for women only there was a curious hush and patter of bare feet, till the heavy pounding and shuffling of the men's boots broke in again. The whirl of music and dancing in this little kitchen stirred me with an extraordinary effect. The kindliness and merrymaking of these islanders, who, one knows, are full of riot and severity and daring, has a quality and attractiveness that is absent altogether from the life of towns, and makes one think of the life that is shown in the ballads of Scotland.

After the dance the host, who had come in, sang a long English doggerel about a poor scholar who went to Maynooth and had great success in his studies, so that he was praised by the bishop. Then he went home for his holiday, and a young woman who had great riches asked him into her parlour and told him it was no fit life for a fine young man to be a priest, always saying Mass for poor people, and that he would have a right to give up his Latin and get married to herself. He refused her offers and went back to his college. When he was gone she went to the justice in great anger, and swore an oath against him that he had seduced her and left her with child. He was brought back for his trial, and he was in risk to be degraded and hanged, when a man rode up on a horse and said it was himself was the lover of the lady, and the father of her child.

Then they told me about an old man of eighty years, who is going to spend the winter alone on

Inishvickillaun, an island six miles from this village. His son is making canoes and doing other carpenter's jobs on this island, and the other children have scattered also; but the old man refuses to leave the island he has spent his life on, so they have left him with a goat, and a bag of flour and stack of turf.

I have just been to the weaver's, looking at his loom and appliances. The host took me down to his cottage over the brow of the village, where some young men were finishing the skeleton of a canoe; and we found his family crowded round a low table on green stools with rope seats, finishing their dinner of potatoes. A little later the old weaver, who looks pale and sickly compared with the other islanders, took me into a sort of outhouse with a damp feeling in the air, where his loom was set up. He showed me how it was worked, and then brought out some pieces of stuff that he had woven. At first I was puzzled by the fine brown colour of some of the material; but they explained it was from selected wools of the black or mottled sheep that are common here, and are so variegated that many tints of grey or brown can be had from their fleeces. The wool for the flannel is sometimes spun on this island; sometimes it is given to women in Dunquin, who spin it cheaply for so much a pound. Then it is woven, and finally the stuff is sent to a mill in Dingle to be cleaned and dressed before it is given to a tailor in Dingle to be made up for their own use. Such cloth is not cheap, but is of wonderful quality and strength. When I came out of the weaver's, a little sailing smack was anchored in the sound, and someone on board her was blowing a horn. They told me she was the French boat, and as I went back to my cottage I could see many canoes hurrying out to her with their cargoes of lobsters and crabs.

I have left the island again. I walked round the cliffs in the morning, and then packed my bag in my room, several girls putting their heads Into the little window while I did so, to say it was a great pity I was not staying on for another week or a fortnight. Then the men went off with my bag in a heavy shower, and I waited a minute or two while the little hostess buttered some bread for my lunch, and tied it up in a clean handkerchief of her own. Then I bid them good-bye, and set off down to the slip with three girls, who came with me to see that I did not go astray among the innumerable paths. It was still raining heavily, so I told them to put my cape, which they were carrying, over their heads. They did so with delight, and ran down the path before me, to the great amusement of the islanders. At the head of the cliff many people were standing about to bid me good-bye and wish me a good voyage.

The wind was in our favour, so the men took in their oars after rowing for about a quarter of a mile and lay down in the bottom of the canoe, while one man ran up the sail, and the host steered with an oar. At Dunquin the host hired me a dray, without springs, kissed my hand in farewell, and I was driven away.

I have made my way round the foot of Dingle Bay and up the south coast to a cottage where I often lodge. As I was resting in a ditch some time in the afternoon, on a lonely mountain road, a little girl came along with a shawl over her head. She stopped in front of me and asked me where I was going, and then after a little talk: 'Well, man, let you come,' she said; 'I'm going your road as well as you.' I got up and we started. When I got tired of the hill I mounted, and she ran along beside me for several miles, till we fell in with some people cutting turf and she stopped to talk to them.

Then for a while my road ran round an immense valley of magnificent rich turf bog, with mountains all round, and bowls where hidden lakes were lying bitten out of the cliffs.

As I was resting again on a bridge over the Behy where Diarmuid caught salmon with Grania, a man stopped to light his pipe and talk to me. 'There are three lakes above,' he said, 'Coomacarra, Coomaglaslaw and Coomasdhara; the whole of this place was in a great state in the bad times. Twenty years ago they sent down a 'mergency man to lodge above by the lake and serve processes on the people, but the people were off before him and lay abroad in the heather. Then, in the course of a piece, a night came, with great rain out of the heavens, and my man said: "I'll get them this night in their own beds, surely." Then he let call the peelers — they had peelers waiting to mind him — and down they come to the big steppingstones they have above for crossing the first river coming out of the lakes; my man going in front to cross over, and the water was high up covering the Stones. Then he gave two leps or three, and the peelers heard him give a great shriek down in the flood. They went home after — what could they do? — and the 'mergency man was found in the sea stuck in a net.¹

I was singularly pleased when I turned up the boreen at last to this cottage where I lodge, an looked down through a narrow gully to Dingle Bay. The people bade me welcome when came in, the old woman kissing my hand.

There is no village near this cottage, yet many farms are scattered on the hills near it; and as the people are in some ways a leading family, many men and women look in to talk or tell stories, or to buy a few pennyworth of sugar or starch. Although the main road passes a few hundred yards to the west, this cottage is well known also to the race of local tramps who move from one family to another in some special neighbourhood or barony. This evening, when I came in, a little old man in a tall hat and long brown coat was sitting up on the settle beside the fire, and intending to spend, one could see, a night or more in the place.

I had a great deal to tell the people at first of my travels in different parts of the county, to the Blasket Islands — which they can see from here — Corkaguiney and Tralee; and they had news to tell me also of people who have married or died since I was here before, or gone away, or come back from America. Then I was told that the old man, Dermot (or Darby, as he is called in English), was the finest story-teller in Iveragh; and after a while he told us a long story in Irish, but spoke so rapidly and indistinctly — he had no teeth — that I could understand but few passages. When he had finished I asked him where he had heard the story.

'I heard it in the city of Portsmouth,' he said. 'I worked there for fifteen years, and four years in Plymouth, and a long while in the hills of Wales; twenty-five years in all I was working at the other side; and there were many Irish in it, who would be telling stories in the evening, the same as we are doing here. I heard many good stories, but what can I do with them now and I an old lisping fellow, the way I can't give them out like a ballad?'

When he had talked a little more about his travels, and a bridge over the Severn, that he thought the greatest wonder of the world, I asked him if he remembered the Famine.

'I do,' he said. 'I was living near Kenmare, and many's the day I saw them burying the corpses in the ditch by the road. It was after that I went to England, for this country was ruined and destroyed. I heard there was work at that time in Plymouth; so I went to Dublin and took a boat that was going to England; but it was at a place called Liverpool they put me on shore, and then I had to walk to Plymouth, asking my way on the road. In that place I saw the soldiers after coming back from the Crimea, and they all broken and maimed.'

A little later, when he went out for a moment, the people told me he beats up and down between Killorglin and Ballinskelligs and the Inny river, and that he is a particular crabby kind of man, and will not take anything from the people but coppers and eggs.

'And he's a wasteful old fellow with all,' said the woman of the house, 'though he's eighty years old or beyond it, for whatever money he'll get one day selling his eggs to the coastguards, he'll spend it the next getting a drink when he's thirsty, or keeping good boots on his feet.'

From that they began talking of misers, and telling stories about them.

'There was an old woman,' said one of the men, 'living beyond to the east, and she was thought to have a great store of money. She had one daughter only, and in the course of a piece a young lad got married to her, thinking he'd have her fortune. The woman died after — God be merciful to her! — and left the two of them as poor as they were before. Well, one night a man that knew them was passing to the fair of Puck, and he came in and asked would they give him a lodging for that night. They gave him what they had and welcome; and after his tea, when they were sitting over the fire — the way we are this night — the man asked them how they were so poor-looking, and if the old woman had left nothing behind her.

'"Not a farthing did she leave," said the daughter.

"And did she give no word or warning or message in her last moments?" said the man.

'"She did not," said the daughter, "except only that I shouldn't comb out the hair of her poll and she dead."

'"And you heeded her?" said the man.

'"I did, surely," said the daughter.

"'Well," said the man, "to-morrow night when I'm gone let the two of you go down the Relic (the graveyard), and dig up her coffin and look in her hair and see what it is you'll find in it."

"'We'll do that," said the daughter, and with that they all stretched out for the night.

'The next evening they went down quietly with a shovel and they dug up the coffin, and combed through her hair, and there behind her poll they found her fortune, five hundred pounds, in good notes and gold.'

'There was an old fellow living on the little hill beyond the graveyard,' said Danny-boy, when the man had finished, 'and he had his fortune some place hid in his bed, and he was an old weak fellow, so that they were all watching him to see he wouldn't hide it away. One time there was no one in it but himself and a young girl, and the old fellow slipped out of his bed and went out of the door as far as a little bush and some stones. The young girl kept her eye on him, and she made sure he'd hidden something in the bush; so when he was back in his bed she called the people, and they all came and looked in the bushes, but not a thing could they find. The old man died after, and no one ever found his fortune to this day.'

'There were some young lads a while since,' said the old woman, 'and they went up of a Sunday and began searching through those bushes to see if they could find anything, but a kind of a turkey-cock came up out of the stones and drove them away.'

'There was another old woman,' said the man of the house, 'who tried to take down her fortune into her stomach. She was near death, and she was all day stretched in her bed at the corner of the fire. One day when the girl was tinkering about, the old woman rose up and got ready a little skillet that was near the hob and put something into it and put it down by the fire, and the girl watching her all the time under her oxter, not letting on she seen her at all. When the old woman lay down again the girl went over to put on more sods on the fire, and she got a look into the skillet, and what did she see but sixty sovereigns. She knew well what the old woman was striving to do, so she went out to the dairy and she got a lump of fresh butter and put it down into the skillet, when the woman didn't see her do it at all. After a bit the old woman rose up and looked into the skillet, and when she saw the froth of the butter she thought it was the gold that was melted. She got back into her bed — a dark place, maybe — and she began sipping and sipping the butter till she had the whole of it swallowed. Then the girl made some trick to entice the skillet away from her, and she found the sixty sovereigns in the bottom and she kept them for herself.'

By this time it was late, and the old woman brought over a mug of milk and a piece of bread to Darby at the settle, and the people gathered at their table for their supper; so I went into the little room at the end of the cottage where I am given a bed.

When I came into the kitchen in the morning, old Darby was still asleep on the settle, with his coat and trousers over him, a red night-cap on his head, and his half-bred terrier, Jess, chained with a chain he carries with him to the leg of the settle.

'That's a poor way to lie on the bare board,' said the woman of the house, when she saw me looking at him; 'but when I filled a sack with straw for him last night he wouldn't have it at all.'

While she was boiling some eggs for my breakfast, Darby roused up from his sleep, pulled on his trousers and coat, slipped his feet into his boots and started off, when he had eaten a few mouthfuls, for another house where he is known, some five miles away.

Afterwards I went out on the cnuceen, a little hill between this cottage and the sea, to watch the people gathering carragheen moss, a trade which is much followed in this district during the spring tides of summer. I lay down on the edge of the cliff, where the heathery hill comes to an end and the steep rocks begin. About a mile to the west there was a long headland, 'Feakle Callaigh' ('The Witch's Tooth '), covered with mists, that blew over me from time to time with a swish of rain, followed by sunshine again. The mountains on the other side of the bay were covered, so I could see nothing but the strip of brilliant sea below me, thronged with girls and men up to their waists in the water, with a hamper in one hand and a stick in the other, gathering the moss, and talking and laughing loudly as they worked. The long frill of dark golden rocks covered with seaweed, with the asses and children slipping about on it, and the bars of silvery light breaking through on the further inlets of the bay, had the singularly brilliant loveliness one meets everywhere in Kerry.

When the tide began to come in I went down one of the passes to the sea, and met many parties of girls and old men and women coming up with what they had gathered, most of them still wearing the clothes that had been in the sea, and were heavy and black with salt water. A little further on I met Danny-boy and we sat down to talk.

'Do you see that sandy head?' he said, pointing out to the east, 'that is called the Stooks of the Dead Women; for one time a boat came ashore there with twelve dead women on board her, big ladies with green dresses and gold rings, and fine jewelleries, and a dead harper or fiddler along with them. Then there are graves again in the little hollow by the cnuceen, and what we call them is the Graves of the Sailors; for some sailors, Greeks or great strangers, were washed in there a hundred years ago, and it is there that they were buried.'

Then we began talking of the carragheen he had gathered and the spring tides that would come again during the summer. I took out my diary to tell him the times of the moon, but he would hardly listen to me. When I stopped, he gave his ass a cut with his stick, 'Go on now,' he said; 'I wouldn't believe those almanacs at all; they do not tell the truth about the moon.'

The greatest event in West Kerry is the horse-fair, known as Puck Fair, which is held in August. If one asks anyone, many miles east or west of Killorglin, when he reaped his oats or sold his pigs or heifers, he will tell you it was four or five weeks, or whatever it may be, before or after Puck. On the main roads, for many days past, I have been falling in with tramps and trick characters of all kinds, sometimes single and sometimes in parties of four or five, and as I am on the roads a great deal I have often met the same persons several days in succession — one day perhaps at Ballinskelligs, the next day at Feakle Callaigh, and the third in the outskirts of Killorglin.

Yesterday cavalcades of every sort were passing from the west with droves of horses, mares, jennets, foals and asses, with their owners going after them in flat or railed carts, or riding on ponies.

The men of this house — they are going to buy a horse — went to the fair last night, and I followed at an early hour in the morning. As I came near Killorglin the road was much blocked by the latest sellers pushing eagerly forward, and early purchasers who were anxiously leading off their young horses before the roads became dangerous from the crush of drunken drivers and riders.

Just outside the town, near the first public-house, blind beggars were kneeling on the pathway, praying with almost Oriental volubility for the souls of anyone who would throw them a coin.

'May the Holy Immaculate Mother of Jesus Christ,' said one of them, 'intercede for you in the hour of need. Relieve a poor blind creature, and may Jesus Christ relieve yourselves in the hour of death. May He have mercy, I'm saying, on your brothers and fathers and sisters for evermore.'

Further on stalls were set out with cheap cakes and refreshments, and one could see that many houses had been arranged to supply the crowds who had come in. Then I came to the principal road that goes round the fair-green, where there was a great concourse of horses, trotting and walking and galloping; most of them were of the cheaper class of animal, and were selling, apparently to the people's satisfaction, at prices that reminded one of the time when fresh meat was sold for threepence a pound. At the further end of the green there were one or two rough shooting galleries, and a number of women — not very rigid, one could see — selling, or appearing to sell, all kinds of trifles: a set that come in, I am told, from towns not far away. At the end of the green I turned past the chapel, where a little crowd had just carried in a man who had been killed or badly wounded by a fall from a horse, and went down to the bridge of the river, and then back again into the main slope of the town. Here there were a number of people who had come in for amusement only, and were walking up and down, looking at each other — a crowd is as exciting as champagne to these lonely people, who live in long glens among the mountains — and meeting with cousins and friends. Then, in the three-cornered space in the middle of the town, I came on Puck himself a magnificent he-goat (Irish puc), raised on a platform twenty feet high, and held by a chain from each horn, with his face down the road. He is kept in this position, with a few cabbages to feed on, for three days, so that he may preside over the pig-fair and the horse-fair and the day of winding up.

At the foot of this platform, where the crowd was thickest, a young ballad-singer was howling a ballad in honour of Puck, making one think of the early Greek festivals, since the time of which, it is possible, the goat has been exalted yearly in Killorglin.

The song was printed on a green slip by itself. It ran:

A NEW SONG ON THE GREAT PUCK FAIR.

By JOHN PURCELL.

All young lovers that are fond of sporting,
pay attention for a while,
I will sing you the praises of Puck Fair,
and I'm sure it will make you smile;
Where the lads and lassies coming gaily to Killorglin can be seen,
To view the Puck upon the stage, as our hero dressed in green.

Chorus.

And hurra for the gallant Puck so gay,
For he is a splendid one
Wind and rain don't touch his tail,
For his hair is thirty inches long.

Now it is on the square he's erected with all colours grand and gay;
There's not a fair throughout Ireland, but Puck Fair it takes the sway,
Where you see the gamblers in rotation, trick — o'-the-loop and
other games,

The ballad-singers and the wheel-of-fortune and the shooting-gallery
for to take aim.

>   Chorus.

Where is the tyrant dare oppose it?
Our old customs we will hold up still,
And I think we will have another —
That is, Home Rule and Purchase Bill.

Now, all young men that are not married,
next Shrove can take a wife,
For before next Puck Fair we will have Home Rule,
and then you will be settled down in life.
Now the same advice I give young girls for to get
married and have pluck.
Let the landlords see that you defy them when
coming to Fair of Puck.

>   Cead Mile Failte to the Fair of Puck.

When one makes the obvious elisions, the lines are not so irregular as they look, and are always sung to a measure: yet the whole, in spite of the assonance, rhymes, and the 'colours grand and gay,' seems pitifully remote from any good spirit of ballad-making.

Across the square a man and a woman, who had a baby tied on her back, were singing another ballad on the Russian and Japanese War, in the curious method of antiphony that is still sometimes heard in the back streets of Dublin. These are some of the verses:

Man.

Now provisions are rising, 'tis sad for to state,
The flour, tea and sugar, tobacco and meat;
But, God help us I poor Irish, how must we stand the test

Ambo.

If they only now stop the trade of commerce.

Woman.

Now the Russians are powerful on sea and on land;
But the Japs they are active, they will them command,
Before this war is finished I have one word to say,

Ambo.

There will be more shot and drowned than in the Crimea.

Man.

Now the Japs are victorious up to this time,
And thousands of Russians I hear they are dying.

Etc., etc.

And so it went on with the same alternation of the voices through seven or eight verses; and it was curious to feel how much was gained by this simple variation of the voices.

When I passed back to the fair-green, I met the men I am staying with, and went off with them under an archway, and into a back yard to look at a little two-year-old filly that they had bought and left for the moment in a loose box with three or four young horses. She was prettily and daintily shaped, but looked too light, I thought, for the work she will be expected to do. As we came out again into the road, an old man was singing an out-spoken ballad on women in the middle of the usual crowd. Just as we passed it came to a scandalous conclusion; and the women scattered in every direction, shrieking with laughter and holding shawls over their mouths.

At the corner we turned into a public-house, where there were men we knew, who had done their business also; and we went into the little alcove to sit down quietly for a moment. 'What will you take, sir,' said the man I lodge with, 'a glass of wine?'

I took beer and the others took porter; but we were only served after some little time, as the house was thronged with people.

The men were too much taken up with their bargains and losses to talk much of other matters; and before long we came out again, and the son of the house started homewards, leading the new filly by a little halter of rope.

Not long afterwards I started also. Outside Killorglin rain was coming up over the hills of Glen Car, so that there was a strained hush in the air, and a rich, aromatic smell coming from the bog myrtle, or boggy shrub, that grows thickly in this place. The strings of horses and jennets scattered over the road did not keep away a strange feeling of loneliness that seems to hang over this brown plain of bog that stretches from Carrantuohull to Cuchulain's House.

Before I reached the cottage dense torrents of

rain were closing down through the glens, and driving in white sheets between the little hills that are on each side of the way.

One morning in autumn I started in a local train for the first stage of my journey to Dublin, seeing the last of Macgillicuddy's Reeks, that were touched with snow in places, Dingle Bay and the islands beyond it. At a little station where I changed trains, I got into a carriage where there was a woman with her daughter, a girl of about twenty, who seemed uneasy and distressed. Soon afterwards, when a collector was looking at our tickets, I called out that mine was for Dublin, and as soon as he got out the woman came over to me.

'Are you going to Dublin?' she said.

I told her I was.

'Well,' she went on, 'here is my daughter going there too; and maybe you'd look after her, for I'm getting down at the next station. She is going up to a hospital for some little complaint in her ear, and she has never travelled before, so that she's lonesome in her mind.'

I told her I would do what I could, and at the next station I was left alone with my charge, and one other passenger, a returned American girl, who was on her way to Mallow, to get the train for Queenstown. When her mother was lost sight of the young girl broke out into tears, and the returned American and myself had trouble to quiet her.

'Look at me,' said the American. 'I'm going off for ten years to America, all by myself, and I don't care a rap.'

When the girl got quiet again, the returned American talked to me about scenery and politics and the arts — she had been seen off by her sisters in bare feet, with shawls over their heads — and the life of women in America.

At several stations girls and boys thronged in to get places for Queenstown, leaving parties of old men and women wailing with anguish on the platform. At one place an old woman was seized with such a passion of regret, when she saw her daughters moving away from her for ever, that she made a wild rush after the train and when I looked out for a moment I could see her writhing and struggling on the platform, with her hair over her face, and two men holding her by the arms.

Two young men had got into our compartment for a few stations only, and they looked on with the greatest satisfaction.

'Ah,' said one of them, 'we do have great sport every Friday and Saturday, seeing the old women howling in the stations.'

When we reached Dublin I left my charge for a moment to see after my baggage, and when I came back I found her sitting on a luggage barrow, with her package in her hand, crying with despair because several cabmen had refused to let her into their cabs, on the pretext that they dreaded infection.

I could see they were looking out for some rich tourist with his trunks, as a more lucrative fare; so I sent for the head-porter, who had charge of the platform. When the porter arrived we chose a cab, and I saw my charge driven off to her hospital, sitting on the front seat, with her handkerchief to her eyes.

For the last few days — I am staying in the Kerry cottage I have spoken of already — the people have been talking of horse-races that were to be held on the sand, not far off and this morning I set out to see them with the man and woman of the house and two of their neighbours. Our way led through a steep boreen for a quarter of a mile to the edge of the sea, and then along a pathway between the cliffs and a straight grassy hill. When we had gone some distance the old man pointed out a slope in front of us, where, he said, Diarmuid had done his tricks of rolling the barrel and jumping over his spear, and had killed many of his enemies. He told me the whole story, slightly familiarized in detail, but not very different from the version everyone knows. A little further on he pointed across the sea to our left — just beyond the strand where the races were to be run — to a neck of sand where, he said, Oisin was called away to the Tir-na-nOg.

'The Tir-na-nOg itself,' he said, 'is below that sea, and a while since there were two men out in a boat in the night-time, and they got stuck outside some way or another. They went to sleep then, and when one of them wakened up he looked down into the sea, and he saw the Tir-na-nOg and people walking about, and side-cars driving in the squares.'

Then he began telling me stories of mermaids — a common subject in this neighbourhood.

'There was one time a man beyond of the name of Shee,' he said, 'and his master seen a mermaid on the sand beyond combing her hair, and he told Shee to get her. "I will," said Shee, "if you'll give me the best horse you have in your stable." "I'll do that," said the master. Then Shee got the horse, and when he saw the mermaid on the sand combing her hair, with her covering laid away from her, he galloped up, when she wasn't looking, and he picked up the covering and away he went with it. Then the waves rose up behind him and he galloped his best, and just as he was coming out at the top of the tide the ninth wave cut off his horse behind his back, and left himself and the half of his horse and the covering on the dry land. Then the mermaid came in after her covering, and the master got married to her, and she lived with him a long time, and had children — three or four of them. Well, in the wind-up, the master built a fine new house, and when he was moving into it, and clearing the things out, he brought down an old hamper out of the loft and put it in the yard. The woman was going about, and she looked into the hamper, and she saw her covering hidden away in the bottom of it. She took it out then and put it upon her and went back into the sea, and her children used to be on the shore crying after her. I'm told from that day there isn't one of the Shees can go out in a boat on that bay and not be drowned.'

We were now near the sandhills, where a crowd was beginning to come together, and booths were being put up for the sale of apples and porter and cakes. A train had come in a little before at a station a mile or so away, and a number of the usual trick characters, with their stock-in-trade, were hurrying down to the sea. The roulette man passed us first, unfolding his table and calling out at the top of his voice:

Come play me a game of timmun and tup,
The more you puts down the more you takes up.

'Take notice, gentlemen, I come here to spend a fortune, not to make one. Is there any sportsman in a hat or a cap, or a wig or a waistcoat, will play a go with me now? Take notice, gentlemen, the luck is on the green.'

The races had to be run between two tides while the sand was dry, so there was not much time to be lost, and before we reached the strand the horses had been brought together, ridden by young men in many variations of jockey dress. For the first race there was one genuine race-horse, very old and bony, and two or three young horses belonging to farmers in the neighbourhood. The start was made from the middle of the crowd at the near end of the strand, and the course led out along the edge of the sea to a post some distance away, back again to the starting-point, round a post, and out and back once more.

When the word was given the horses set off in a wild helter-skelter along the edge of the sea, with crowds cheering them on from the sandhills. As they got small in the distance it was not easy to see which horse was leading, but after a sort of check, as they turned the post, they began nearing again a few yards from the waves, with the old race-horse, heavily pressed, a good length ahead. The stewards made a sort of effort to clear the post that was to be circled, but without much success, as the people were wild with excitement. A moment later the old race-horse galloped into the crowd, twisted too suddenly, something cracked and jolted, and it limped out on three legs, gasping with pain. The next horse could not be stopped, and galloped out at the wrong end of the crowd for some little way before it could be brought back, so the last horses set off in front for the final lap.

The lame race-horse was now mobbed by onlookers and advisers, talking incoherently.

'Was it the fault of the jock?' said one man.

'It was not,' said another, 'for Michael (the owner) didn't strike him, and if it had been his fault, wouldn't he have broken his bones?'

'He was striving to spare a young girl had run out in his way,' said another. 'It was for that he twisted him.'

'Little slut!' said a woman; 'what did she want beyond on the sand?'

Many remedies were suggested that did not sound reassuring, and in the end the horse was led off in a hopeless condition. A little later the race ended with an easy win for the wildest of the young horses. Afterwards I wandered up among the people, and looked at the sports. At one place a man, with his face heavily blackened, except one cheek and eye — an extraordinary effect — was standing shots of a wooden ball behind a board with a large hole in the middle, at three shots a penny. When I came past half an hour afterwards he had been hit in the mouth — by a girl some one told me — but seemed as cheerful as ever.

On the road, some little distance away, a party of girls and young men were dancing polkas to the music of a melodeon, in a cloud of dust. When I had looked on for a little while I met some girls I knew, and asked them how they were getting on.

'We're not getting on at all,' said one of them, 'for we've been at the races for two hours, and we've found no beaux to go along with us.'

When the horses had all run, a jennet race was held, and greatly delighted the people, as the jennets — there were a number of them — got scared by the cheering and ran wild in every direction. In the end it was not easy to say which was the winner, and a dispute began which nearly ended in blows. It was decided at last to run the race over again the following Sunday after Mass, so everyone was satisfied.

The day was magnificently bright, and the ten miles of Dingle Bay were wonderfully brilliant behind the masses of people, and the canvas booths, and the scores of upturned shafts. Towards evening I got tired taking or refusing the porter my friends pressed on me continually, so I wandered off from the racecourse along the path where Diarmuid had tricked the Fenians.

Later in the evening news had been coming in of the doings in the sandhills, after the porter had begun to take effect and the darkness had come on.

'There was great sport after you left,' a man said to me in the cottage this evening. 'They were all beating and cutting each other on the shore of the sea. Four men fought together in one place till the tide came up on them, and was like to drown them; but the priest waded out up to his middle and drove them asunder. Another man was left for dead on the road outside the lodges, and some gentleman found him and had him carried into his house, and got the doctor to put plasters on his head. Then there was a red-headed fellow had his finger bitten through, and the postman was destroyed for ever.'

'He should be,' said the man of the house, 'for Michael Patch broke the seat of his car into three halves on his head.'

'It was this was the cause of it all,' said Danny-boy: 'they brought in porter east and west from the two towns you know of, and the two porters didn't agree together, and it's for that the people went raging at the fall of night.'

I have been out to Bolus Head, one of the finest places I have met with. A little beyond Ballinskelligs the road turns up the side of a steep mountainy hill where one sees a brilliant stretch of sea, with many rocks and islands — Deenish, Scariff the Hog's Head, and Dursey far away. As I was sitting on the edge of the road an old man came along and we began to talk. He had little English, but when I tried him in Irish we got on well, though he did not follow any Connaught forms I let slip by accident. We went on together, after a while, to an extraordinary straggling village along the edge of the hill. At one of the cottages he stopped and asked me to come in and take a drink and rest myself. I did not like to refuse him, we had got so friendly, so I followed him in, and sat down on a stool while his wife — a much younger woman — went into the bedroom and brought me a large mug of milk. As I was drinking it and talking to the couple, a sack that was beside the fire began to move slowly, and the head of a yellow, feverish-looking child came out from beneath it, and began looking at me with a heavy stare. I asked the woman what ailed it, and she told me it had sickened a night or two before with headache and pains all through it; but she had not had the doctor, and did not know what was the matter. I finished the milk without much enjoyment, and went on my way up Bolus Head and then back to this cottage, wondering all the time if I had the germs of typhus in my blood.

Last night, when I got back to the cottage, I found that another 'travelling man' had arrived to stay for a day or two; but he was hard of hearing and a little simple in his head, so that we had not much talk. I went to bed soon after dark and slept till about two o'clock in the morning, when I was awakened by fearful screams in the kitchen. For a moment I did not know where I was; then I remembered the old man, and I jumped up and went to the door of my room. As I opened it I heard the door of the family room across the kitchen opening also, and the frightened whispers of the people. In a moment we could hear the old man, who was sleeping on the settle, pulling himself out of a nightmare, so we went back to our beds.

In the morning the woman told me his story:

'He was living above on a little hillside,' she said, 'in a bit of a cabin, with his sister along with him. Then, after a while, she got ailing in her heart, and he got a bottle for her from the doctor, and he'd rise up every morning before the dawn to give her a sup of it. She got better then, till one night he got up and measured out the spoonful, or whatever it was, and went to give it to her, and he found her stretched out dead before him. Since that night he wakes up one time and another, and begins crying out for Maurya — that was his sister — and he half in his dreams. It was that you heard in the night, and indeed it would frighten any person to hear him screaming as if he was getting his death.'

When the little man came back after a while, they began asking him questions till he told his whole story, weeping pitiably. Then they got him to tell me about the other great event of his life also, in the rather childish Gaelic he uses.

He had once a little cur-dog, he said, and he knew nothing of the dog licence; then one day the peelers — the boys with the little caps — asked him into the barracks for a cup of tea. He went in cheerfully, and then they put him and his little dog into the lock-up till some one paid a shilling for him and got him out.

He has a stick he is proud of, bound with pieces of leather every few inches — like one I have seen with a beggar in Belmullet. Since the first night he has not had nightmare again, and he lies most of the evening sleeping on the settle, and in the morning he goes round among the houses, getting his share of meal and potatoes.

I do not think a beggar is ever refused in Kerry. Sometimes, while we are talking or doing something in the kitchen, a man walks in without saying anything and stands just inside the door, with his bag on the floor beside him. In five or ten minutes, when the woman of the house has finished what she is doing, she goes up to him and asks: 'Is it meal or flour?' 'Flour,' says the man. She goes into the inner room, opens her sack, and comes back with two handfuls. He opens his bag and takes out a bundle carefully tied up in a cloth or handkerchief; he opens this again, and usually there is another cloth inside, into which the woman puts her flour. Then the cloths are carefully knotted together by the corners, put back in the bag, and the man mutters a 'God bless you,' and goes on his way.

The meal, flour and potatoes that are thus gathered up are always sold by the beggar, and the money is spent on porter or second-hand clothes, or very occasionally on food when he is in a neighbourhood that is not hospitable. The buyers are usually found among the coastguards' wives, or in the little public-houses on the roadside.

'Some of these men,' said the woman of the house, when I asked her about them, 'will take their flour nicely and tastily and cleanly, and others will throw it in anyway, and you'd be sorry to eat it afterwards.'

The talk of these people is almost bewildering. I have come to this cottage again and again, and I often think I have heard all they have to say, and then some one makes a remark that leads to a whole new bundle of folk-tales, or stories of wonderful events that have happened in the barony in the last hundred years. Tonight the people were unusually silent, although several neighbours had come in, and to make conversation I said something about the bull-fights in Spain that I had been reading of in the newspapers. Immediately they started off with stories of wicked or powerful bulls, and then they branched off to clever dogs and all the things they have done in West Kerry, and then to mad dogs and mad cattle and pigs — one incident after another, but always detailed and picturesque and interesting.

I have come back to the north of Dingle, leaving Tralee late in the afternoon. At the station there was a more than usually great crowd, as there had been a fair in the town and many people had come in to make their Saturday purchases. A number of messenger boys with parcels from the shops in the town were shouting for the owners, using many familiar names, Justin MacCarthy, Hannah Lynch and the like. I managed to get a seat on a sack of flour beside the owner, who had other packages scattered under our feet. When the train had started and the women and girls — the carriage was filled with them — had settled down into their places, I could see I caused great curiosity, as it was too late in the year for even an odd tourist, and on this line everyone is known by sight.

Before long I got into talk with the old man next me, and as soon as I did so the women and girls stopped their talk and leaned out to hear what we were saying.

He asked first if I belonged to Dingle, and I told him I did not.

'Well,' he said, 'you speak like a Kerry man, and you're dressed like a Kerry man, so you belong to Kerry, surely.'

I told him I was born and bred in Dublin, and that I had travelled in many places in Ireland and beyond it.

'That's easy said,' he answered, 'but I'd take an oath you were never beyond Kerry to this day.'

Then he asked sharply: 'What do you do?'

I answered something about my wanderings in Europe, and suddenly he sat up, as if a new thought had come to him.

'Maybe you're a wealthy man?' he said. I smiled complacently.

'And about thirty-five?'

I nodded.

'And not married?'

'No.'

'Well then,' he said, 'you're a damn lucky fellow to be travelling the world with no one to impede you.'

Then he went on to discuss the expenses of travelling.

'You'll likely be paying twenty pounds for this

trip,' he said, 'with getting your lodging and buying your tickets, till you're back in the city of Dublin?'

I told him my expenses were not so heavy.

'Maybe you don't drink so,' said his wife, who was near us, 'and that way your living wouldn't be so costly at all.'

An interruption was made by a stop at a small station and the entrance of a ragged ballad-singer, who sang a long ballad about the sorrows of mothers who see all their children going away from them to America.

Further on, when the carriage was much emptier, a middle-aged man got in, and we began discussing the fishing season, Aran fishing, hookers, nobbies, and mackerel. I could see, while we were talking, that he, in his turn, was examining me with curiosity. At last he seemed satisfied.

'Begob,' he said, 'I see what you are; you're a fish-dealer.'

It turned out that he was the skipper of a trawler, and we had a long talk, the two of us and a local man who was going to Dingle also.

'There was one time a Frenchman below,' said the skipper, 'who got married here and settled down and worked with the rest of us. One day we were outside in the trawler, and there was a French boat anchored a bit of a way off. "Come on," says Charley — that was his name — "and see can we get some brandy from that boat beyond." "How would we get brandy," says I, "when we've no fish, or meat, or cabbages or a thing at all to offer them?" He went down below then to see what he could get. At that time there were four men only working the trawler, and in the heavy season there were eight. Well, up he comes again and eight plates under his arm. "There are eight plates," says he, "and four will do us; so we'll take out the other four and make a swap with them for brandy." With that he set the eight plates on the deck and began walking up and down and looking on them.

'"The devil mend you," says I. "Will you take them up and come on, if you're coming?"

'"I will," says he, "surely. I'm choicing out the ones that have pictures on them, for it's that kind they do set store on?"'

Afterwards we began talking of boats that had been upset during the winter, and lives that had been lost in the neighbourhood.

'A while since,' said the local man, 'there were three men out in a canoe, and the sea rose on them. They tried to come in under the cliff but they couldn't come to land with the greatness of the waves that were breaking. There were two young men in the canoe, and another man was sixty, or near it. When the young men saw they couldn't bring in the canoe, they said they'd make a jump for the rocks, and let her go without them, if she must go. Then they pulled in on the next wave, and when they were close in the two young men jumped on to a rock, but the old man was too stiff, and he was washed back again in the canoe. It came on dark after that, and all thought he was drowned, and they held his wake in Dunquin. At that time there used to be a steamer going in and out trading in Valentia and Dingle and Cahirciveen, and when she came into Dingle, two or three days after, there was my man on board her, as hearty as a salmon. When he was washed back he got one of the oars, and kept her head to the wind; then the tide took him one bit and the wind took him another, and he wrought and he wrought till he was safe beyond in Valentia. Wasn't that a great wonder?' Then as he was ending his story we ran down into Dingle.

Often, when one comes back to a place that one's memory and imagination have been busy with, there is a feeling of smallness and disappointment, and it is a day or two before one can renew all one's enjoyment. This morning, however, when I went up the gap between Croagh Martin and then back to Slea Head, and saw Inishtooskert and Inishvickillaun and the Great Blasket Island itself, they seemed ten times more grey and wild and magnificent than anything I had kept in my memory. The cold sea and surf, and the feeling of winter in the clouds, and the blackness of the rocks, and the red fern everywhere, were a continual surprise and excitement.

Here and there on my way I met old men with tail-coats of frieze, that are becoming so uncommon. When I spoke to them in English, they shook their heads and muttered something I could not hear; but when I tried Irish they made me long speeches about the weather and the clearness of the day.

In the evening, as I was coming home, I got a glimpse that seemed to have the whole character of

Corkaguiney — a little line of low cottages with yellow roofs, and an elder tree without leaves beside them, standing out against a high mountain that seemed far away, yet was near enough to be dense and rich and wonderful in its colour.

Then I wandered round the wonderful forts of Fahan. The blueness of the sea and the hills from Carrantuohill to the Skelligs, the singular loneliness of the hillside I was on, with a few choughs and gulls in sight only, had a splendour that was almost a grief in the mind.

I turned into a little public-house this evening, where Maurice — the fisherman I have spoken of before — and some of his friends often sit when it is too wild for fishing. While we were talking a man came in, and joined rather busily in what was being said, though I could see he was not belonging to the place. He moved his position several times till he was quite close to me, then he whispered: 'Will you stand me a medium, mister? I'm hard set for money this while past.' When he had got his medium he began to give me his history. He was a journeyman tailor who had been a year or more in the place, and was beginning to pick up a little Irish to get along with. When he had gone we had a long talk about the making of canoes and the difference between those used in Connaught and Munster.

'They have been in this country,' said Maurice, 'for twenty or twenty-five years only, and before that we had boats; a canoe will cost twelve pounds, or maybe thirteen pounds, and there is one old man beyond who charges fifteen pounds. If it is well done a canoe will stand for eight years, and you can get a new skin on it when the first one is gone.' I told him I thought canoes had been in Connemara since the beginning of the world.

'That may well be,' he went on, 'for there was a certain man going out as a pilot, up and down into Clare, and it was he made them first in this place. It is a trade few can learn, for it is all done within the head; you will have to sit down and think it out, and then make up when it is all ready in your mind.'

I described the fixed thole-pins that are used in Connaught — here they use two freely moving thole-pins, with the oar loose between them, and they jeered at the simplicity of the Connaught system. Then we got on the relative value of canoes and boats.

'They are not better than boats,' said Maurice, 'but they are more useful. Before you get a heavy boat swimming you will be wet up to your waist, and then you will be sitting the whole night like that; but a canoe will swim in a handful of water, so that you can get in dry and warm the whole night. Then there will be seven men in a big boat and seven shares of the fish; but in a canoe there will be three men only and three shares of the fish, though the nets are the same in the two.'

After a while a man sang a song, and then we began talking of tunes and playing the fiddle, and I told them how hard it was to get any sound out of one in a cottage with a floor of earth and a thatched roof over you.

'I can believe that,' said one of the men. 'There was a man a while since went into Tralee to buy a fiddle; and when he went into the shop an old fiddler followed him into it, thinking maybe he'd get the price of a pint. Well, the man was within choicing the fiddles, maybe forty of them, and the old fiddler whispered to him to take them out into the air, "for there's many a fiddle would sound well in here wouldn't be worth a curse outside," says he; so he was bringing them out and bringing them out till he found a good one among them.'

This evening, after a day of teeming rain, it cleared for an hour, and I went out while the sun was setting to a little cove where a high sea was running. As I was coming back the darkness began to close in except in the west, where there was a red light under the clouds. Against this light I could see patches of open wall and little fields of stooks, and a bit of laneway with an old man driving white cows before him. These seemed transfigured beyond any description.

Then I passed two men riding bare-backed towards the west, who spoke to me in Irish, and a little further on I came to the only village on my way. The ground rose towards it, and as I came near there was a grey bar of smoke from every cottage going up to the low clouds overhead, and standing out strangely against the blackness of the mountain behind the village.

Beyond the patch of wet cottages I had another stretch of lonely roadway, and a heron kept flapping in front of me, rising and lighting again with many lonely cries that made me glad to reach the little public-house near Smerwick.

www.ingramcontent.com/pod-product-compliance
Lightning Source LLC
Chambersburg PA
CBHW020129010526
44115CB00008B/1039